Hexagons, Diamonds, Triangles, and More

Hexagons, Diamonds, Triangles, and More

Skill-Building Techniques for 60-Degree Patchwork

Kelly Ashton

Martingale®
Create with Confidence

Dedication

This book is dedicated to quiltmakers past, present, and future. We make quilts for many reasons: for function, fun, or creative challenge; to wrap up in on a chilly evening or to adorn a wall; as a gift of love or to make a statement; and on and on! No matter the reason, the creative energy and love that is generated and expended in quiltmaking is therapeutic and makes the world a better place.

Hexagons, Diamonds, Triangles, and More:
Skill-Building Techniques for 60-Degree Patchwork
© 2014 by Kelly Ashton

Martingale®
19021 120th Ave. NE, Ste. 102
Bothell, WA 98011-9511 USA
ShopMartingale.com

Printed in China

19 18 17 16 15 14   8 7 6 5 4 3 2 1

**Library of Congress Cataloging-in-Publication Data
is available upon request.**

ISBN: 978-1-60468-369-1

Mission Statement

Dedicated to providing quality products and service to inspire creativity.

Credits

PRESIDENT AND CEO: Tom Wierzbicki

EDITOR IN CHIEF: Mary V. Green

DESIGN DIRECTOR: Paula Schlosser

MANAGING EDITOR: Karen Costello Soltys

ACQUISITIONS EDITOR: Karen M. Burns

TECHNICAL EDITOR: Rebecca Kemp Brent

COPY EDITOR: Tiffany Mottet

PRODUCTION MANAGER: Regina Girard

COVER AND INTERIOR DESIGNER: Connor Chin

PHOTOGRAPHER: Brent Kane

ILLUSTRATOR: Christine Erikson

Contents

Introduction

My first introduction to a 60° quilt came in the late 1960s when I was a child of about eight or nine. My paternal grandmother, Edna Bertha Steven Ashton (or Mamo, as I called her), showed me a lovely Grandmother's Flower Garden quilt she had made in the 1930s, before I was even a glimmer in my daddy's eye. She made it and "put it away for someday" when she might have a granddaughter to pass it to. I wasn't old enough to truly appreciate all of the work that had gone into that beautiful quilt made from hundreds of little hexagons, but I knew, even then, that it had been lovingly made with me (or at least her imagined version of me) in mind, and I treasured it. My parents carefully wrapped up the quilt and "put it away for someday" when I had a home and family of my own.

I loved school and I was a good student. Though there were really no academic subjects that I didn't like, I was always drawn to math and science. (Yes, I was a geek, and I still am.) I really enjoyed geometry. Drawing shapes with a compass and protractor was fun. I found the logical problem-solving utilizing axioms and theorems both challenging and satisfying. I remember a conversation that I had with my teacher in which I told her how much I enjoyed solving the geometric problems. In the next breath, I told her that, enjoyment aside, I'd likely never use these skills in "real life." Ha! I look back on that conversation now and literally laugh out loud.

Fast-forward more than 30 years, to 2000. I was married with children. My Mamo's quilt was proudly displayed in our family room. I frequently stopped to admire the near-perfect piecing and quilting from so long ago. By then I was a quiltmaker myself, so I decided it was time

Handmade by Edna Bertha Steven Ashton, circa 1935

Notice how carefully Mamo fussy-cut the flowers for the hexagons. Look at those tiny, even hand-quilting stitches!

to explore making a hexagon quilt of my own. I knew that I didn't wish to tackle the tiny hexagons used in Mamo's quilt, and that I wanted to machine piece my quilt top. When I stumbled upon Small Hexagons Plus, template set G by Marti Michell, I was sure I had found exactly what I needed to begin my hexagon adventure. I was right!

The accuracy and size options of the template set allowed me to explore working with hexagons and related shapes with confidence. I learned to construct blocks requiring Y-seams (also known as set-in seams) with ease and near perfection. As I became more confident, I began to explore drafting shapes that worked in concert with the shapes in the set. As my proficiency developed and I wanted more size options, I learned to draft hexagons and the other shapes in sizes that yielded the block size I desired. Pure creative freedom!

In many ways, this book mirrors my own 60° journey. First, it will introduce you to some very interesting shapes that work together in a multitude of ways to create quilt blocks. There are patterns in the book for all the shapes in a variety of sizes, and instructions for making your own templates. Additionally, there are suggestions for ready-made templates and tools that are available in today's broad market of useful tools for quilters, including the template set from Marti Michell that I found so helpful. Plus, there are a lot of block designs and setting options within these pages.

I offer tips for preparing fabric, cutting pieces, sewing Y-seams, and pressing the seam allowances. I discuss tools and supplies that have worked well for me, and why I like them. However, I know that "there's more than one way to skin a cat," as Mamo used to say, so I offer my ideas and opinions as a place for you to begin

My first hexagon quilt: "Grandmother's Bouquet." Machine pieced and quilted by Kelly Ashton, 2000.

your journey while encouraging you to try other approaches as ideas come to mind. You'll find the methods that work best for you.

I include information on setting options, explanations for finding the dimensions of pattern pieces, and instructions for two introductory projects to help you master Y-seams. Finally, there is a gallery of quilts to inspire you.

Sixty-degree blocks and quilts are not "instant gratification" projects. Creating blocks with Y-seams takes a little more time (truly, just a little more!) than making blocks with strip piecing and other quick techniques. However, mastering the technique of sewing Y-seams adds another tool to your box of quiltmaking skills, and this tool will open up opportunities for creating many interesting blocks that are impossible to make any other way. I love the feelings of accomplishment and satisfaction that came when I made these blocks and quilts, and I believe they are worth the extra effort. I hope you will, too!

Getting Started
with 60 Degrees

Frequently Asked Questions

Whenever I lecture or teach a workshop project using 60° shapes and sewing Y-seams, there are recurring questions. Here are answers to some questions you may be asking, too.

Q: Do I have to be a geometry whiz (or even like geometry) to use this book?

A: No! The geometry is all worked out, so you can simply enjoy making quilts with these interesting shapes. But who knows? By the time you've played your way through the book, you may have a new-found love for geometry.

Q: Do I have to do math computations to use this book?

A: The only math computations are the ones that allow you to figure finished sizes of blocks and quilts. I have made the math very simple, and I've given you examples. See "Calculating Shape Dimensions" on page 66.

Q: I've never sewn Y-seams before. Is this a difficult technique to master?

A: No! If it were, I wouldn't be doing it. Y-seams are not difficult at all, especially when you follow the step-by-step instructions given on pages 25–27.

Q: Do all of the blocks in this book require sewing Y-seams?

A: No. Though most of the blocks do require Y-seams, there are some that do not.

Q: Must I make templates in order to create the blocks in this book?

A: Yes and no. Many of the blocks can be made using purchased templates that are readily available in today's market (see "Patchwork Cutting Guide" on page 21). However, there are a few shapes in some of these blocks for which no ready-made templates are available; for those, handmade templates are a must. Simple instructions for making your own templates are found on page 17.

Q: Do I have to draft patterns to make these blocks?

A: No. The patterns for every block in this book have been included (see pages 29–59), and a variety of templates are available for purchase that will allow you to make many blocks in this book without ever having to make a template yourself, if that is your preference.

The 60-Degree Group of Shapes

If you're not familiar with the group of shapes defined by 60° angles, I am pleased to introduce you to hexagons, diamonds, and equilateral triangles. If you've had some acquaintance, I hope to further your friendship with this amazing and versatile group of polygons (a fancy geometry word for two-dimensional shapes with straight sides).

For the blocks in this book, I have drafted a group of 13 individual shapes, all derived by subdividing a hexagon. Each shape is available in two or three sizes that work together in a multitude of ways to create interesting blocks of various sizes. I began with a set of three proportional hexagons that I call primary (4"

sides), secondary (2" sides), and tertiary (1" sides). I hope to give you a sense of the relationship of these shapes to their hexagon of origin and to each other through pictures and description. Through combinations of these shapes, a plethora of interesting quilt blocks can be formed. And from those blocks, you'll make some fabulous quilts!

Measuring Up

All of the measurements given are based on the finished dimensions of the shape *without* seam allowances.

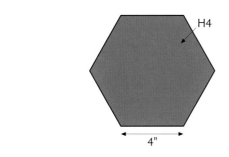

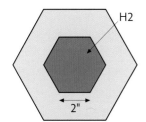

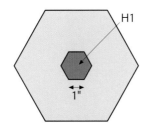

Hexagon. The regular hexagon (for simplicity, it's referred to in the book simply as "hexagon") is a six-sided shape with sides of equal length and equal internal angles that always measure 120°. I abbreviate this shape as H, followed by a number denoting the length of each side.

The primary hexagon for the shapes in this book measures 4" along each side. The distance from the center of this hexagon to any of its corner points is also 4". The secondary hexagon is half as large, with sides that measure 2", which is also the distance from its center to any corner point. The tertiary hexagon is, again, half as large, measuring just 1".

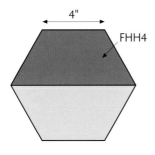

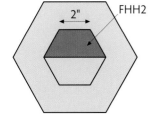

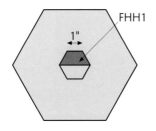

Flat Half Hexagon. The flat half hexagon (FHH) is created by drawing a straight line from one corner point of the hexagon to its opposite point. It's used as a component of several blocks in this book. It can also be used in a quilt to create a straight outer edge. Flat half hexagons can be created from each of the hexagons: primary, secondary, and tertiary.

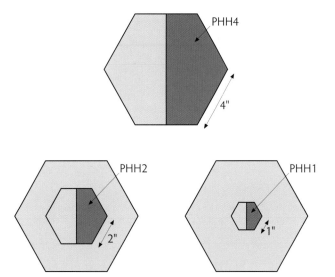

Pointy Half Hexagon. The pointy half hexagon (PHH) is created by drawing a straight line from the midpoint of one side of the hexagon to the midpoint of the opposite side. Pointy half hexagons can be created from each hexagon size and are used in several of the book's blocks. Like the flat half hexagon, they can also be used to give a quilt a straight outer edge.

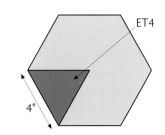
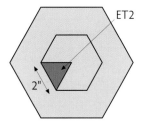
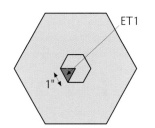

Equilateral Triangle. The equilateral triangle (ET) has three sides of equal length and three equal internal angles, each 60°. To create an equilateral triangle from a hexagon, draw a straight line from each point of the hexagon to its opposite point; each of the six sections is an equilateral triangle. The side length of the equilateral triangle is equivalent to the side length of the original hexagon. It is used in many blocks, and can also fill spaces within quilt layouts.

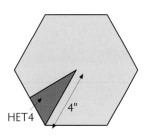
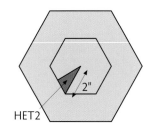
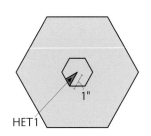

Half Equilateral Triangle. The half equilateral triangle (HET) is created by drawing a line from one point of the equilateral triangle to the midpoint of the opposite side, creating a 90° angle at the base of the resulting triangle. The half equilateral triangle is sometimes used in blocks, and its 90° angle allows it to fill spaces and create a straight outer edge or a 90° corner for a quilt.

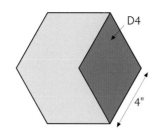

Diamond. The 60° diamond (D) is formed by drawing a straight line from every other outer point to the center point of the hexagon. The lengths of the diamond's four sides are equal. The internal angles of the diamond's two sharp points are 60°; the two wide internal angles are 120°. There is an important relationship between 60° diamonds and equilateral triangles: a 60° diamond can be created from two equilateral triangles, joined at their bases. Diamonds are frequent components of the blocks in this book, and can also be used as fillers in a quilt setting.

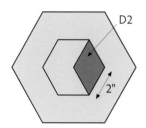

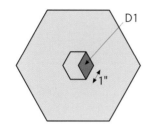

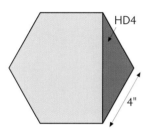

Half Diamond. The half diamond (HD) is formed by drawing a straight line between the sharp points of a diamond. The half diamond is sometimes used in blocks and can be used to create a straight edge in a quilt.

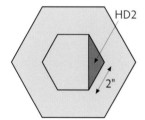

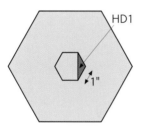

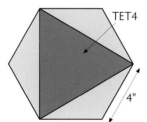

Tipsy Equilateral Triangle. The tipsy equilateral triangle (TET) is formed by drawing three straight lines inside the hexagon, joining every other corner. The tipsy equilateral triangle is used with three half diamonds from the same hexagon to create a pieced hexagon that can be used as a stand-alone block or block component. The pieced hexagon also makes an interesting setting unit in quilts.

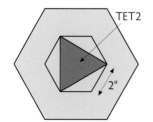

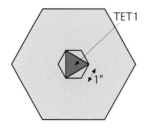

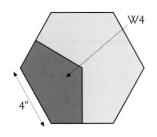

Wedge. The wedge (W) is one-third of a hexagon. It is created by drawing a straight line from the center point of the hexagon to the midpoint of every other side of the hexagon.

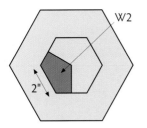
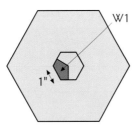

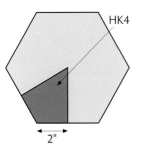
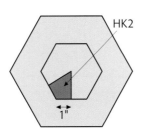

Kite. Kites can be derived from two places inside the hexagon. The shapes are the same, but the sizes are different.

Hexagon Kite. Like an equilateral triangle, the hexagon kite (HK) is one-sixth of a hexagon, but its base encompasses a corner, rather than a side, of the hexagon. It is created by drawing a straight line from the midpoints of adjacent sides to the center point of the hexagon. The short sides of the hexagon kite are half the length of the original hexagon's side.

Triangle Kite. The triangle kite (TK) is one-third of an equilateral triangle. To draft it, you must first draw an equilateral triangle; then, draw straight lines from the center point of the triangle to the midpoints of two adjacent sides. The long sides of a triangle kite are half the length of the original hexagon's side.

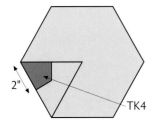
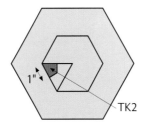

Little Details

Because the tertiary hexagon is so small, a shape derived from it may be too small to be practically useful. That's the case for the kites, petals, and flat triangles, each of which has been drafted from only the primary and secondary hexagons.

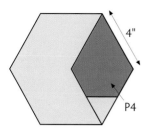 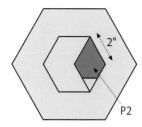

Petal. The petal (P) is formed by taking the diamond derived from one hexagon and subtracting from one of its tips the equilateral triangle from the next smaller hexagon.

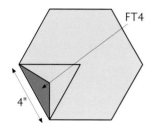 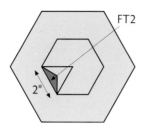

Flat Triangle. The flat triangle (FT) is formed indirectly from the hexagon, but directly from the equilateral triangle. It's one-third of an equilateral triangle, formed by drawing a straight line from the center point of the equilateral triangle to two adjacent corners. It's exactly the same shape as the half diamond, but its different origin gives it a different size.

Getting Ready

My dad used to say, "You'll never regret taking the time to gather the right tools for the task!" For quiltmakers, finding the right tool has never been easier than now, when available tools allow us to be more efficient, more accurate, and have more fun. I'll discuss the tools that I have found useful, but remember that there are many other tools available. I invite you to use my preferences as a starting point as you travel the 60° path, and then explore other options to find the perfect tools for your preferences.

When I took my first quilting class, rotary cutters, rulers, and mats had only recently entered the quiltmaking scene. Hot new techniques included rotary cutting squares and rectangles as well as strip piecing and subcutting quilt-block sections from strip sets. If you also began your quiltmaking journey since the advent of the rotary cutter, you may have little or no experience in making and using plastic templates to cut your patchwork pieces.

With the varied shapes and angles used for the blocks in this book, templates are a must. Thankfully, you don't have to resort to the method of our grandmothers: making a template from the cardboard of a cereal box and then cutting each patchwork piece individually with scissors. Instead, you'll use templates made from heavy plastic or acrylic along with a rotary cutter to efficiently and accurately cut patches from fabric strips.

You can make templates for each of the shapes from the patterns beginning on page 86. For *some* of the shapes, making your own templates is the only option, as there are no manufactured templates available. However, when commercially made templates are available, they are a wonderful convenience. Consult the "Patchwork Cutting Guide" on page 21 for specifics regarding shapes that are available for purchase.

Templates

Making templates from template plastic is not a difficult task, but accuracy and attention to detail are important.

Template-Making Supplies

Begin by gathering your materials.

Template plastic. I prefer EZ Quilting's Extra Thick Template Plastic by Wrights because the plastic is transparent, so it's easy to see the lines that need to be traced. It is also thick and sturdy, making the templates easy to handle and, with extreme caution, possible to rotary cut around.

Permanent marker. Choose a fine-tipped permanent marking pen. I prefer Sharpie Ultra Fine permanent markers; they maintain their very fine marking tip and last a long time.

Rulers. Standard 6" and 12" rulers are essential in my toolbox. I use the 6" more often when tracing templates, but it is convenient to have both available.

Fabric grippers. There are many anti-slip products on the market for placing on the bottom of rulers and templates to prevent movement while cutting. I've tried many, and prefer Fabric Grips by Collins—little adhesive-backed sandpaper circles that adhere to the bottom of the ruler or template. They are thin, so they don't cause distortion and movement of the template when cutting multiple fabric layers at once. Their biggest disadvantage is that they aren't transparent, so I take care in deciding where on the template to place them. I use fabric grippers on both purchased and handmade templates.

Paper scissors. Once you've traced your template pattern onto the heavy-duty plastic, you will need to cut out the template. *Don't use your good fabric scissors to cut template plastic*, or they won't be your "good scissors" any longer! I don't recommend using a rotary cutter to cut the heavy-duty template plastic; the plastic is so thick that the force required could be very dangerous. Instead, use a quality pair of utility scissors to cut out the template.

Hole punch. Reference holes punched at the template corners help ensure seam-line accuracy. A ¹⁄₁₆" hole punch is optional, but I think it's worth the expense for the smooth, uniform holes it creates. As an alternative, you can use a corkboard pushpin to make the hole.

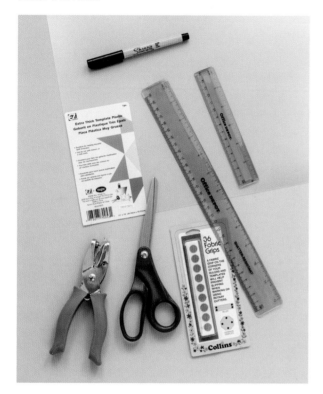

Supplies for making templates

Making Your Own Templates

Follow these steps to make accurate templates.

1. Familiarize yourself with the patterns beginning on page 86. The outermost line is the cutting line; once the template is cut out, the edge of the template becomes the cutting line for the fabric pieces. The outer line has been blunted at some corners; when piecing, the blunted corners eliminate bulk in areas where several points converge. Ultimately, this allows the quilt block to lie much flatter.

   The inner line, ¼" inside the cutting line, is the stitching line. This line defines the actual size and

shape of the finished patchwork piece. There is also a suggested grain line for each pattern. Transfer the grain line to the template, and write the name and/or abbreviation of the piece on the template.

2. To make it more manageable, roughly cut a piece of template plastic slightly larger than the template shape you're about to trace.

3. Place a fabric gripper on the underside of the plastic to keep it from sliding as you trace. Place the plastic over the pattern.

4. Align the ruler slightly to one side of the line to be traced, so the drawn line will lie exactly on top of the printed line. Using the fine-tipped pen, draw the cutting, sewing, and grain lines and write the name on the template. Use the utility scissors to cut out the template on the cutting line.

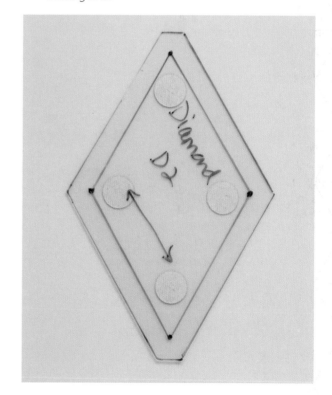

A finished template, with fabric grippers

5. Add reference holes at the corners by using the hole punch to make an opening at each corner of the seam line. By inserting a marker through the holes, you'll be able to mark reference points

on the fabric pieces as an aid for stitching accurate seams and knowing where to begin and end the Y-seams.

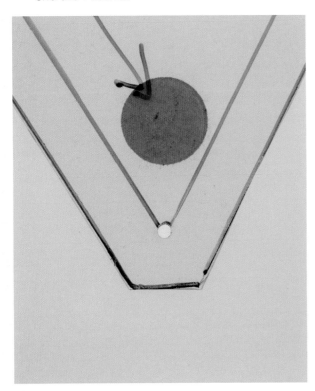

A seam-line reference hole

6. Add additional fabric grippers to the bottom of the template as needed. I usually place one near each corner of a template. If the template is large, I also add one at the center.

Manufactured Templates

Many rulers and acrylic templates are designed for use with a rotary cutter, and they can be extremely useful in making the blocks in this book. You can find individual acrylic templates for cutting hexagons, equilateral triangles, 60° diamonds, and related shapes under many brand names. Some products are sized by the finished side length of the shape, while others are sized by the finished height or width of the shape; familiarize yourself with the product before purchasing to be sure it will produce the size you're expecting.

A Fitting Choice

If you wish to purchase ready-made templates to use in making many of the blocks in this book, I recommend Small Hexagons Plus, template set G by Marti Michell. It includes nine shapes. By making the remaining templates yourself, you will have a full complement of templates to use for the blocks in this book and beyond.

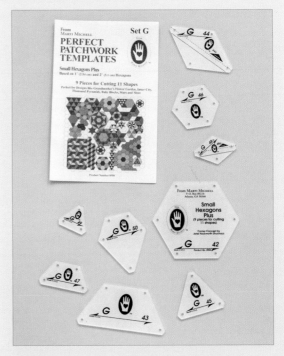

Purchased templates that work well with this book's blocks

Other useful tools include a multisize hexagon ruler and an equilateral (60°) triangle ruler. I recommend the Multiple Size Hexagon Ruler by Marti Michell because it includes cutting lines for a hexagon with 4" finished sides, the primary hexagon used for the blocks in this book. Several equilateral-triangle rulers on the market would work well, too; look for one that includes cutting lines for equilateral triangles with 4", 2", and 1" finished sides.

As with handmade templates, add fabric grippers to the underside of manufactured templates and rulers to minimize slippage while cutting.

Fabric Sizing

Each of the fabric shapes used in creating the blocks in this book will have at least two bias edges (edges that do not fall on the fabric's straight of grain). In order to stabilize the fabric and decrease the possibility of distortion, I strongly recommend adding sizing to the fabric before cutting. Use either spray starch or Mary Ellen's Best Press Non-Starch Alternative, which is my personal favorite, because I like the body and fabric stability it provides and it doesn't flake as spray starch can. I also appreciate that it's nonaerosol and it comes in a variety of scents—or no scent at all!

Extra Benefits

When I first began making quilts, I prewashed every piece of fabric before I used it. As I became busier, I found myself looking for an alternative to that time-consuming step; I'm very pragmatic in my approach to quiltmaking. I've now found that spraying and pressing my fabrics has a dual purpose.

I place a piece of inexpensive bleached muslin on top of my ironing board, and then spritz the quilting fabric with Mary Ellen's Best Press. I don't saturate the fabric, but I spray it generously enough to dampen the fibers. Sometimes, as I spray the fabric, I can literally see the fabric shrink! Next, I use a dry iron on the cotton setting and press the fabric until dry. I am convinced that I've shrunk my fabric as much as if I'd washed and dried it.

With the bleached muslin on my ironing board, I can also see whether a fabric is bleeding. If it is, I set it aside for further evaluation and treatment, in hopes that I'll be able to use it safely in my quilt project.

Fabric and Thread

I recommend beginning your 60° journey with batiks or quilter's cottons for your early projects, then moving on to flannels as your comfort in working with Y-seams grows. Fabrics other than quilter's cottons may cause variations in seam allowances that affect the accuracy of your piecing; see "Y-Seams? Why Not!" on page 25 for more.

Selecting a good piecing thread is also an important part of quiltmaking. Look for long-staple cotton threads. Typically, 50-weight thread is used for piecing, but keep in mind that the actual thickness of 50-weight may vary between manufacturers. I prefer fine 3-ply thread for strength in a thread that takes a minimum of space in the turn of the fabric (see page 25); my favorite is 60-weight Presencia cotton. My second favorite thread is 50-weight Aurifil 2-ply cotton thread.

Some ideal threads for piecing

Cutting Your Patchwork Pieces

While the thick acrylic used in purchased templates is best for rotary cutting, with extra caution, it's also possible to use your handmade templates with a rotary cutter. In the interest of safety, I recommend using a Klutz Glove by Fons and Porter to protect your nondominant hand while rotary cutting. In addition, you will need the following items.

Rotary cutter. I strongly recommend a 28 mm blade for cutting these shapes. Larger cutters (45 or 60 mm) can be awkward when cutting the smaller pieces, creating inaccuracies in the cut pieces. The smaller rotary cutter provides better control for greater accuracy.

Rotary-cutting mat. Any rotary-cutting mat will do, but a revolving mat is a plus. Once the initial strips are cut, the revolving mat makes cutting the specific pieces much simpler and the process more efficient.

Rulers. In addition to the handmade and/or purchased templates and specialty rulers, you will need a ruler to cut fabric strips of the prescribed size before subcutting. A 6" x 24" ruler works well if you're cutting strips from full-width fabric. A 6" x 12" ruler is handy for cutting strips from a fat quarter or fat eighth. It will also be very helpful for cutting borders if at least one of your rulers has a 60° reference line.

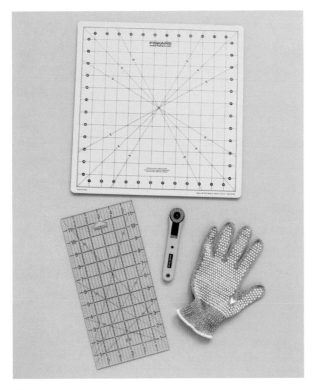

Rotary-cutting tools

Handmade Template Tip

Because template plastic is thin and relatively soft, it's easy to shave a sliver off the edge as you rotary cut. That makes the template inaccurate, in spite of all your care in tracing it.

As an alternative, trace the template onto the fabric with a fine-point removable marker or well-sharpened pencil, lay a rotary-cutting ruler along the traced line (moving it as needed), and cut out the shape. If necessary, you can even cut out the shapes with scissors after tracing.

Using the Patchwork Cutting Guide. Once you've determined the block or blocks you wish to make, you'll begin by cutting fabric strips. The strip size for each of the shapes is listed in the "Patchwork Cutting Guide" on page 21. If you're using directional fabrics for diamonds, half diamonds, kites, or flat triangles, you may wish to control the design direction (horizontal or vertical) as you cut, so alternative cutting options for the fabric strips are given.

Keep the fabric grain line in mind. Whenever possible, every patchwork piece on the outer edge of a quilt block should be cut on the straight of grain, which is more stable than a bias edge. Bias edges stretch and distort more easily than edges cut on the straight of grain. With the angles involved, all of the shapes used in this book will have at least two bias edges, so it isn't always possible to have all the outside edges of the blocks on the straight of grain. Being aware of this fact, and sizing your fabric before cutting, will go a long way toward minimizing patchwork and block distortion.

Stash Math

The values in the table are calculated as accurately as possible, with some margin for error. However, there can always be variations in fabric, tracing, and cutting, so it's a good idea to purchase enough fabric for an additional strip of shapes. Any leftovers go toward building your fabric stash!

Almost all of the shapes are symmetrical, which means that the pieces will have the proper orientation whether you cut them from a flat or folded fabric strip. However, one shape is asymmetrical—the half equilateral triangle. There will be times when you'll need both regular and reversed (mirror-image) half equilateral triangles. To achieve this, simply cut the pieces with the strip folded in half (either right or wrong sides together) so that you are cutting two pieces at once. Each pair of pieces will contain one regular and one reversed piece.

Patchwork Cutting Guide

See "The 60-Degree Group of Shapes" on page 11 for information on shape sizes.

Shape Placement	Template Name	Strip Width	Pieces per 42" Strip	Ready-Made Template Alternative

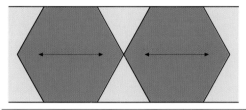

Hexagon

	H4	7½"	4	H4, H2, H1: Multiple Size Hexagon Ruler
	H2	4"	8	H2: Small Hexagons Plus, G42
	H1	2¼"	15	H1: Small Hexagons Plus, G46

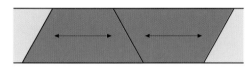

Flat Half Hexagon

	FHH4	4"	5	FHH4: None
	FHH2	2¼"	10	FHH2: Small Hexagons Plus, G43
	FHH1	1⅜"	18	FHH1: Small Hexagons Plus, G47

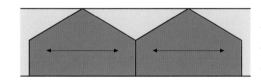

Pointy Half Hexagon

	PHH4	4⅝"	5	None
	PHH2	2⅝"	10	
	PHH1	1⅝"	17	

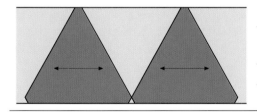

Equilateral Triangle

	ET4	4"	13	ET4, ET2, ET1: any 60°-triangle ruler that includes up to 4" finished sides
	ET2	2¼"	23	ET2: Small Hexagons Plus, G45
	ET1	1⅜"	35	ET1: Small Hexagons Plus, G49

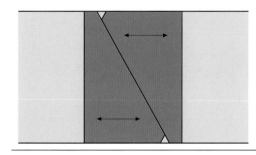

Half Equilateral Triangle

	HET4	4"	24	HET4, HET2, HET1: 60-degree Triangle-Ruler, 2"–6" or 3"–9"
	HET2	2¼"	34	
	HET1	1⅜"	52	

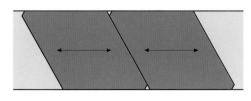

Diamond

	D4	4"	7	D4, D2, D1: 60° Diamond and Triangle Template
	D2	2¼"	14	D2: Small Hexagons Plus, G44
	D1	1⅜"	23	D1: Small Hexagons Plus, G48

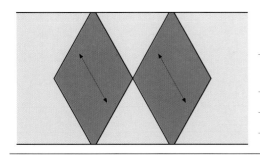

Diamond:
Directional Fabric Cutting, option 1

Template Name	Strip Width	Pieces per 42" Strip	Ready-Made Template Alternative
D4	7½"	8	D4, D2, D1: 60° Diamond and Triangle Template
D2	4"	15	D2: Small Hexagons Plus, G44
D1	2¼"	24	D1: Small Hexagons Plus, G48

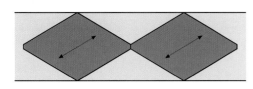

Diamond:
Directional Fabric Cutting, option 2

Template Name	Strip Width	Pieces per 42" Strip	Ready-Made Template Alternative
D4	4⅝"	5	D4, D2, D1: 60° Diamond and Triangle Template
D2	2⅝"	10	D2: Small Hexagons Plus, G44
D1	1⅝"	17	D1: Small Hexagons Plus, G48

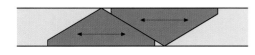

Half Diamond

Template Name	Strip Width	Pieces per 42" Strip	Ready-Made Template Alternative
HD4	2⅝"	7	HD4: None
HD2	1⅝"	13	HD2: Small Hexagons Plus, G44
HD1	1⅛"	20	HD1: Small Hexagons Plus, G48

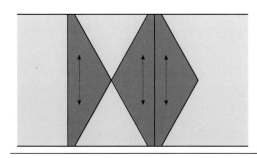

Half Diamond:
Directional Fabric Cutting

Template Name	Strip Width	Pieces per 42" Strip	Ready-Made Template Alternative
HD4	7⅜"	15	HD4: None
HD2	4"	24	HD2: Small Hexagons Plus, G44
HD1	2¼"	36	HD1: Small Hexagons Plus, G48

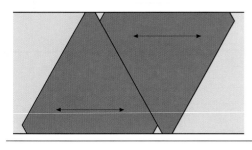

Tipsy Equilateral Triangle

Template Name	Strip Width	Pieces per 42" Strip	Ready-Made Template Alternative
TET4	6½"	8	None
TET2	3½"	15	
TET1	2"	26	

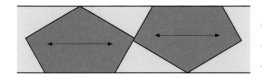

Wedge

Template Name	Strip Width	Pieces per 42" Strip	Ready-Made Template Alternative
W4	4"	6	None
W2	2⅜"	10	
W1	1½"	16	

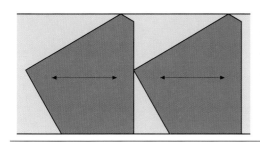

Hexagon Kite

Template Name	Strip Width	Pieces per 42" Strip	Ready-Made Template Alternative
HK4	4"	10	None
HK2	2⅜"	18	

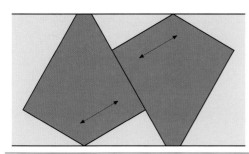

Hexagon Kite: Directional Fabric Cutting

Template Name	Strip Width	Pieces per 42" Strip	Ready-Made Template Alternative
HK4	4⅝"	12	None
HK2	2⅝"	20	

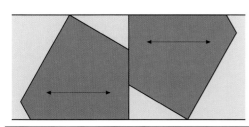

Triangle Kite

Template Name	Strip Width	Pieces per 42" Strip	Ready-Made Template Alternative
TK4	2⅜"	16	None
TK2	1½"	24	

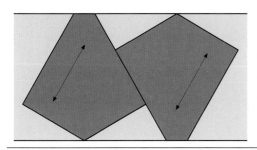

Triangle Kite: Directional Fabric Cutting

Template Name	Strip Width	Pieces per 42" Strip	Ready-Made Template Alternative
TK4	2⅞"	18	None
TK2	1¾"	27	

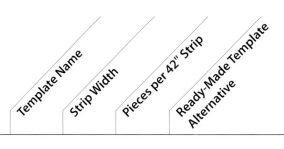

Shape Placement	Template Name	Strip Width	Pieces per 42" Strip	Ready-Made Template Alternative

Petal

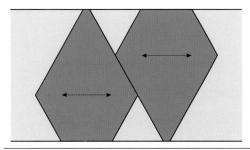

| | P4 | 5¾" | 10 | None |
| | P2 | 3⅛" | 18 | |

Flat Triangle

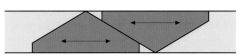

| | FT4 | 1¾" | 11 | None |
| | FT2 | 1⅛" | 19 | |

Flat Triangle: Directional Fabric Cutting

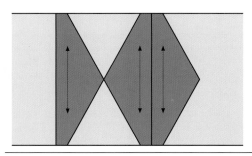

| | FT4 | 4½" | 22 | None |
| | FT2 | 2½" | 34 | |

Convenient Templates

There are some ready-made templates that can be substituted for the handmade templates created from the patterns on pages 86–94. Look for these templates when you shop:

▶ My Favorite Hexagon Ruler by Marti Michell

▶ Perfect Patchwork Templates, Set G, by Marti Michell

▶ 60° Triangle Ruler, large or small, by Marti Michell

▶ Other 60°-triangle rulers with finished side lengths up to 4"

▶ One-derful One Patch 60° Diamond/Triangle Ruler by Marti Michell

Y-Seams? Why Not!

The importance of accurate seams can hardly be overstated, especially when a quilt block contains diverse shapes and angles or employs Y-seams. Like many authors, I recommend a scant ¼" seam allowance, but just what is that? Really, the finished size of the patchwork piece on the right side of the block is more important than the distance between the seam line and the cut edge, so the scant ¼" depends upon three variables: the amount of seam allowance added when cutting, the fabric thickness, and the thread thickness.

We cut patches to include a ¼" seam allowance, but a multitude of variables affect the accuracy of our cutting. Even with perfect cutting accuracy, some seam allowance is lost in the turn of the fabric—the amount of cloth taken up when the patch is pressed over the seam allowances and thread. The turn of the fabric varies with the fabric thickness as well, so a flannel fabric will lose more seam allowance than a fine batik; that means the seam allowances stitched on flannels must be more scant than those on batiks.

The thickness of the thread used to stitch the seam also takes up space inside the turn of the fabric; thicker thread requires a smaller seam allowance in compensation. With only one or two seam allowances, the difference wouldn't amount to much, but the small discrepancy adds up over all the seams in a block.

To ensure accurate finished pieces, the actual seam allowance, as stitched, may need to be one or two thread widths less than ¼" for batiks, and just ⅛" to ³⁄₁₆" for really plush flannels. It's always a good idea to stitch and measure a few sample patches with your chosen fabric and thread before beginning a project.

Sewing Y-Seams by Machine

Most of the blocks in this book use Y-seams, also known as set-in seams. Y-seams are required when three or more patchwork pieces with angles other than 90° converge at one point. Sewing a Y-seam requires that the stitching line stops ¼" from the raw edge of the patch so that the pieces can be shifted, allowing the next piece to be set in.

To explore the process, let's start with a simple Tumbling Block.

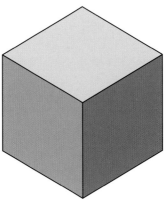

1. Place the pieces right side up in their respective positions. Laying out a block before sewing provides the opportunity to make sure that each patch is in its correct position and orientation, and it provides an opportunity to be sure you like the way each piece looks next to its neighbors before stitching them together. The Tumbling Block clearly illustrates why set-in seams are referred to as "Y-seams"!

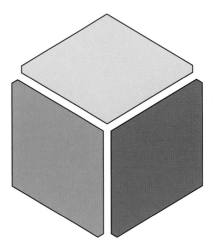

2. Using the reference holes on the template, mark the seam-line intersections on the wrong sides of the patches. These represent the start/stop points for the seams.

3. Place two patches right sides together, using pins to align the reference points. Pin the pieces in place.

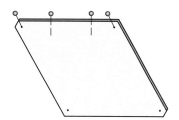

4. Insert the sewing-machine needle at one reference point. Take two stitches forward, backstitch two stitches, and then stitch the seam, stopping at the next reference point. Backstitch two stitches.

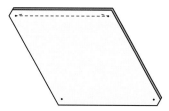

Seams Secure

Backstitching locks the stitches in place at the beginning and end of the seam so that they don't pull out when the patches are shifted to set in the next piece. Many newer, computerized machines have a lock-stitch function, similar to tying a knot at the end of the seam. I don't recommend that function because occasionally it overshoots the end of the seam. If I overshoot when I've backstitched, I can clip one stitch and still have reinforcement of the seam.

5. Open the two pieces you've sewn together and align a third piece with one of the two. Make sure the outside corners and reference points match and pin the piece in place.

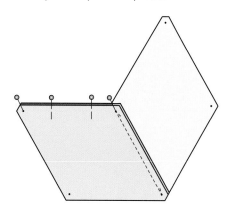

6. Beginning at the outside edge of the block, sew the new patch in place, backstitching at each end to secure the seam. As you near the end of the seam, move the first patch out of the way so that neither the patch nor the seam allowances are caught in the new seam; you'll be sewing through just two layers of fabric.

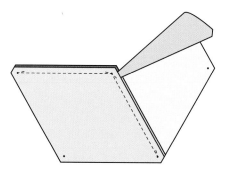

To the Center

I like to stitch all seams from the outside edge of the block toward the block center. This keeps the outside edges even, and keeps everything moving toward the center convergence point.

7. Shift the patches to match the raw edges of the first and third pieces and pin as before. Allow the second patch to fold as you match the reference points. Stitch the seam, remembering to move the rest of the fabric out of the way, and backstitch at each end of the seam.

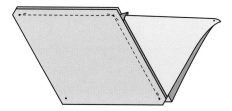

Pressing

My approach to quiltmaking is evident in the way I press seam allowances. Pressing is essential in creating blocks and quilt tops that lie flat and look good. One of the most familiar rules of pressing is to press seam allowances toward the darker fabric. When working with Y-seams, this isn't always possible or practical, and there are contradictory points of view regarding options. One school of thought is to press the seam allowances open; another is to press the seam allowances so they wheel about the center point in a circular fashion. Neither approach is absolutely right or wrong, but there are advantages and disadvantages to each.

Open pressing. Pressing seam allowances open flattens the area around the seam line by distributing the seam allowances evenly to both sides. However, it leaves the line of stitching very vulnerable, as the threads within the seam are not protected; over time, the seam is more likely to be stressed and threads broken than when seam allowances are pressed to one side. Pressing seam allowances open also leaves a space for batting fibers to make their way to the outside of the quilt. I very rarely choose to press seam allowances open.

So, how do I press? The majority of the time, I press the seam allowances to one side, protecting the seams and avoiding a hole between patchwork pieces. My pragmatic bottom line: I use a variety of techniques to achieve the goal of producing blocks, quilt tops, and finished quilts that look as good as possible from the right side of the project. As you're creating blocks, I encourage you to experiment with these different techniques to find your own preferences.

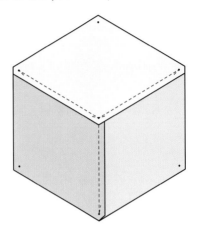

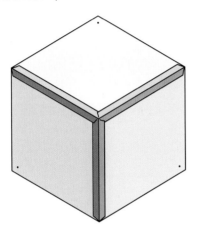

Circular pressing. Pressing seam allowances in a circular fashion distributes the seam allowances around the point of seam convergence where there can be a lot of fabric congestion, but it can leave a hole at the convergence point. The hole may be unnoticeable if the seaming is very well executed, but poor execution can leave the hole quite notice-able and quilting may pull the fabric away from the hole, making it even more obvious. This is true of both hand and machine quilting. Though I do use circular pressing occasionally, it's not a technique I use often.

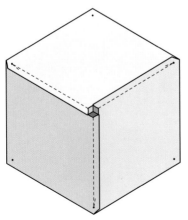

The Blocks

All of the blocks in this book fall into one of four categories: equilateral triangle, hexagon, 60° diamond, or six-pointed star. You will notice that within each category there are simple blocks and compound blocks. The simple designs can be stand-alone blocks, but they are also used as components in compound blocks. A block that is compound is not necessarily *complex* to piece, but it has more pieces and is likely to contain a simple block or two.

As you make fabric choices, be aware of value (a color's relative lightness or darkness) as well as color options. Value contrast within blocks and quilts provides an additional level of visual interest, giving life to the project and drawing the observer's eye. Keep the placement of value and the value of placement in mind as you plan your projects.

You will notice that each block is shown as a line drawing, without color or fill, to illustrate the included pieces and their placement. Then, it is shown with values added in a pulled-apart view, to illustrate how it is constructed. Finally, there is a fully integrated view showing the finished block.

The instructions for each block contain a pair of tables. In the first, the necessary shapes (keyed to the patterns on pages 86–94) are listed, along with the number of each shape to cut for one block. In the second table you'll find specific variations for each block size, expressed in terms of the finished length of one side.

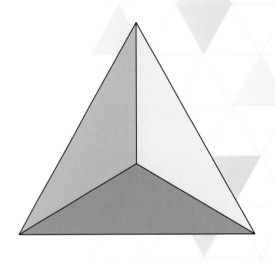

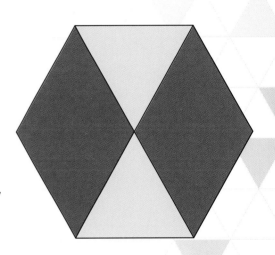

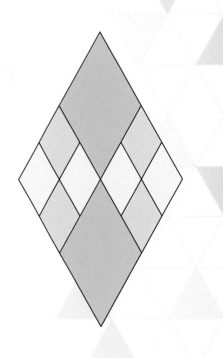

Triangle Blocks ▲

All of these blocks have three sides and three corners, but that doesn't limit their variety.

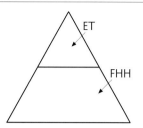

Striped Triangle

The Striped Triangle can be used as a stand-alone block, and you'll find it as a unit in other blocks later in the book. It also makes a very effective pieced border, as you can see in "Two-Color Fair Isle" on page 75.

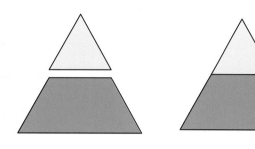

Shape	Number per Block
ET	1 light
FHH	1 dark

Block Size	Patterns to Use
2"	ET1, FHH1
4"	ET2, FHH2
8"	ET4, FHH4

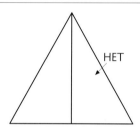

Split Triangle

Shape	Number per Block
HET	2 (Cut 1 regular and 1 reversed from 2 fabrics; see page 20.)

Block Size	Patterns to Use
1"	HET1
2"	HET2
4"	HET4

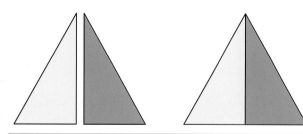

Diamond Triangle

Shape	Number per Block
D	1 dark
ET	2 light

Block Size	Patterns to Use
2"	D1, ET1
4"	D2, ET2
8"	D4, ET4

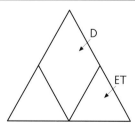
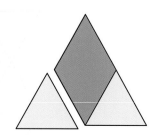
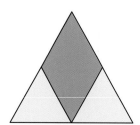

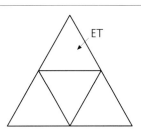

Inset Triangle

Shape	Number per Block
ET	4 (3 dark and 1 light *or* 3 light and 1 dark)

Block Size	Patterns to Use
2"	ET1
4"	ET2
8"	ET4

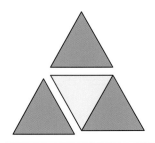
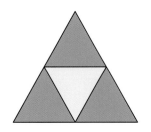

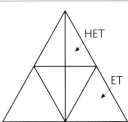

Jester Triangle

Shape	Number per Block
HET	4 (Cut 1 regular and 1 reversed from *each* of 2 fabrics; see page 20.)
ET	2 contrast

Block Size	Patterns to Use
4"	HET2, ET2
8"	HET4, ET4

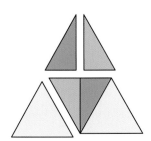
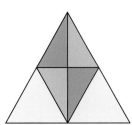

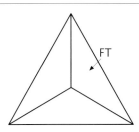

Pyramid

Shape	Number per Block
FT	3 (1 *each* of light, medium, and dark)

Block Size	Patterns to Use
2"	FT2
4"	FT4

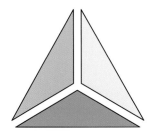
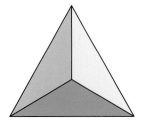

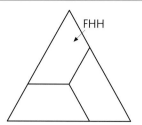

Single-Blade Triangle

Shape	Number per Block
FHH	3 (1 dark and 2 light)

Block Size	Patterns to Use
3"	FHH1
6"	FHH2
12"	FHH4

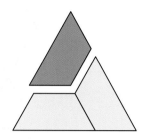
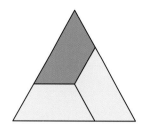

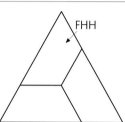

Double-Blade Triangle

The construction of this block is exactly the same as the Single-Blade Triangle block above. The only difference is the value distribution.

Shape	Number per Block
FHH	3 (1 *each* of light, medium, and dark)

Block Size	Patterns to Use
3"	FHH1
6"	FHH2
12"	FHH4

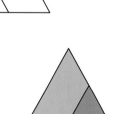

Trilogy

Shape	Number per Block
TK *or* HK	3 (1 dark and 2 light *or* 1 *each* of light, medium, and dark)

Block Size	Patterns to Use
2"	TK2
3½"	HK2
4"	TK4
7"	HK4

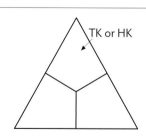

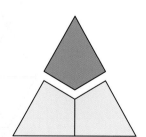
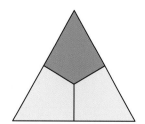

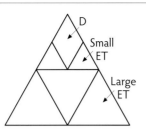

Fractured Triangle

Shape	Number per Block
D	1 dark
Small ET	2 medium
Large ET	3 (1 light and 2 dark matching the D)

Block Size	Patterns to Use
4"	D1, ET1, ET2
8"	D2, ET2, ET4

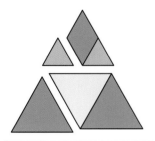
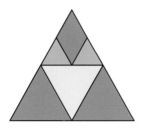

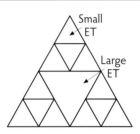

King Tut's Tomb

Shape	Number per Block
Small ET	12 (3 matching the large ET and 9 contrast)
Large ET	1

Block Size	Patterns to Use
4"	ET1, ET2
8"	ET2, ET4

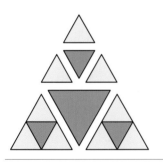
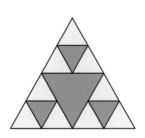

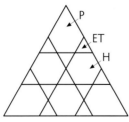

Hexed Triangle

Shape	Number per Block
P	3 light
ET	10 dark
H	3 light

Block Size	Patterns to Use
7"	P2, ET1, H1
14"	P4, ET2, H2

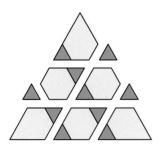
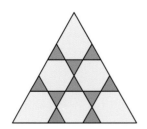

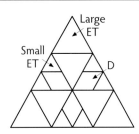

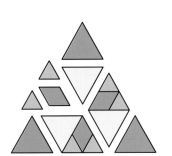
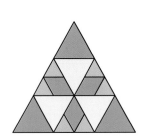

Shape	Number per Block
Small ET	6 medium
Large ET	6 (3 *each* of light and dark)
D	3 dark

Block Size	Patterns to Use
6"	ET1, D1, ET2
12"	ET2, D2, ET4

Hexagon Blocks ⬡

The shapes derived from a hexagon can be reassembled to make pieced hexagons.

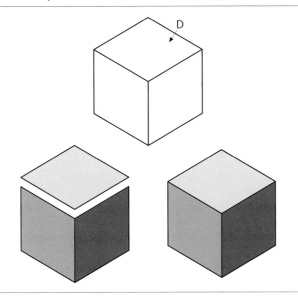

Tumbling Block

Shape	Number per Block
D	3 (1 *each* of light, medium, and dark)

Block Size	Patterns to Use
1"	D1
2"	D2
4"	D4

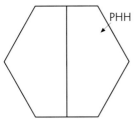

Night and Day Hexagon

Shape	Number per Block
PHH	2 (1 *each* of light and dark)

Block Size	Patterns to Use
1"	PHH1
2"	PHH2
4"	PHH4

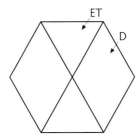

Argyle Hexagon

Shape	Number per Block
D	2 dark
ET	2 light

Block Size	Patterns to Use
1"	D1, ET1
2"	D2, ET2
4"	D4, ET4

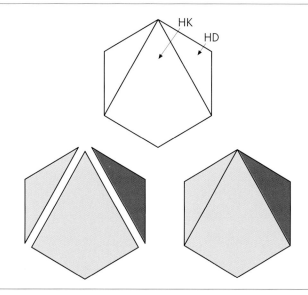

Solo Hexagon

Shape	Number per Block
HK	1 light
HD	2 (1 *each* of light and dark)

Block Size	Patterns to Use
1"	HK2, HD1
2"	HK4, HD2

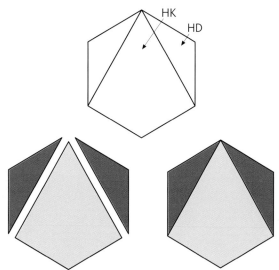

Duet Hexagon

The piecing is exactly the same as Solo Hexagon above; the only difference is that both half diamonds are cut from the contrasting fabric.

Shape	Number per Block
HK	1 light
HD	2 dark

Block Size	Patterns to Use
1"	HK2, HD1
2"	HK4, HD2

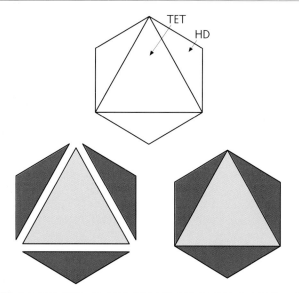

Trio Hexagon

Shape	Number per Block
TET	1 light
HD	3 dark

Block Size	Patterns to Use
1"	TET1, HD1
2"	TET2, HD2
4"	TET4, HD4

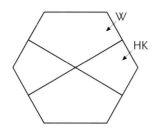

Wedge Hexagon

Shape	Number per Block
W	2 dark
HK	2 light

Block Size	Patterns to Use
2"	W2, HK2
4"	W4, HK4

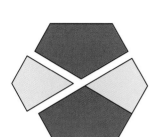 

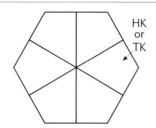

Colonial Garden

Shape	Number per Block
HK or TK	6 (3 each of 2 fabrics) (Use either HK or TK pieces to make the block size of your choice.)

Block Size	Patterns to Use
1¼"	TK2
2"	HK2
2½"	TK4
4"	HK4

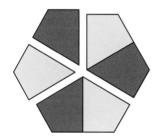 

Spider Web

Use the same 2 fabrics throughout the block, alternating placement.

Shape	Number per Block
ET	6 (3 each of 2 fabrics)
FHH	6 (3 each of 2 fabrics)

Block Size	Patterns to Use
2"	ET1, FHH1
4"	ET2, FHH2
8"	ET4, FHH4

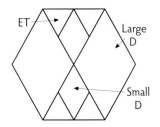

Dash

Shape	Number per Block
ET	4 light
Small D	2 dark
Large D	2 light

Block Size	Patterns to Use
2"	ET1, D1, D2
4"	ET2, D2, D4

 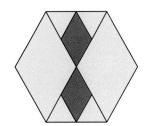

Zigzag

Shape	Number per Block
ET	4 (2 *each* of medium and dark)
D	4 light
FHH	4 (2 *each* of the same 2 ET fabrics)

Block Size	Patterns to Use
2"	ET1, D1, FHH1
4"	ET2, D2, FHH2
8"	ET4, D4, FHH4

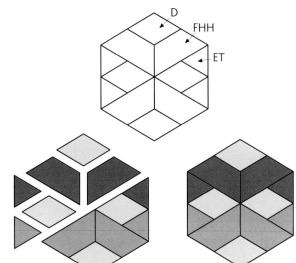

Chain Link

Shape	Number per Block
ET	4 dark
D	4 (2 *each* of medium and dark)
FHH	4 light

Block Size	Patterns to Use
2"	ET1, D1, FHH1
4"	ET2, D2, FHH2
8"	ET4, D4, FHH4

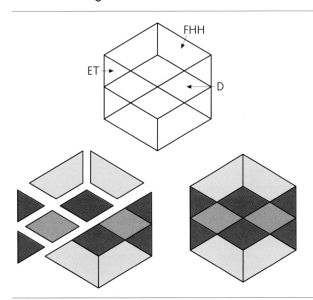

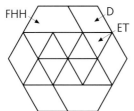
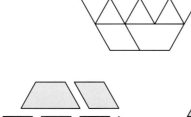
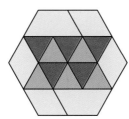

Jacob's Other Ladder

Shape	Number per Block
ET	10 (5 *each* of medium and dark)
D	4 light
FHH	2 light

Block Size	Patterns to Use
2"	ET1, D1, FHH1
4"	ET2, D2, FHH2
8"	ET4, D4, FHH4

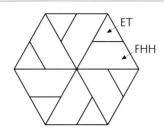

Spinner

Shape	Number per Block
ET	6 light
FHH	6 dark

Block Size	Patterns to Use
2"	ET1, FHH1
4"	ET2, FHH2
8"	ET4, FHH4

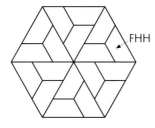

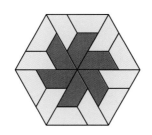

Whirligig

Shape	Number per Block
FHH	18 (12 light and 6 dark)

Block Size	Patterns to Use
3"	FHH1
6"	FHH2
12"	FHH4

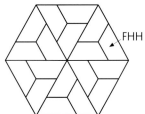

Paddle Wheel

Paddle Wheel is pieced the same way as Whirligig on page 39; the difference is in the placement of color and/or value.

Shape	Number per Block
FHH	18 (6 *each* of 3 fabrics)

Block Size	Patterns to Use
3"	FHH1
6"	FHH2
12"	FHH4

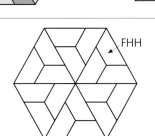

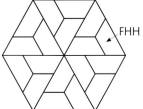

Moonwalk

Moonwalk is another variation of Whirligig on page 39. Shifting the color and value placement gives the block an entirely different look.

Shape	Number per Block
FHH	18 (6 light and 12 dark)

Block Size	Patterns to Use
3"	FHH1
6"	FHH2
12"	FHH4

Triad Hexagon

I love the illusion of a partially covered central triangle created by the piecing of this block.

Shape	Number per Block
Small ET	6 medium
Large ET	3 light
D	3 dark

Block Size	Patterns to Use
2"	ET1, D1, ET2
4"	ET2, D2, ET4

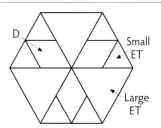

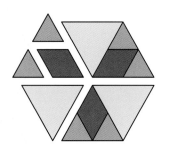

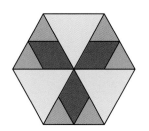

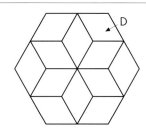

Baby Blocks

Baby Blocks is a great example of "the placement of value and the value of placement." Using light-, medium-, and dark-value fabrics in the same positions in each of the Tumbling Block units creates a three-dimensional perspective.

Shape	Number per Block
D	12 (3 *each* of very light, light, medium, and dark)

Block Size	Patterns to Use
2"	D1
4"	D2
8"	D4

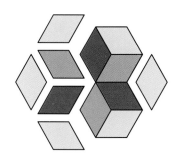
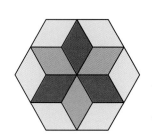

Six-Pointed Star

The Six-Pointed Star is made from the same patchwork pieces as Baby Blocks above. Different color and value placement in this block creates an entirely different look.

Shape	Number per Block
D	12 (6 for star and 6 for background; the 6 star pieces can be all 1 fabric, 3 *each* of 2 fabrics, *or* 1 *each* of 6 fabrics.)

Block Size	Patterns to Use
2"	D1
4"	D2
8"	D4

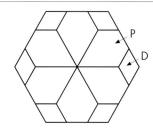

Siberian Squill

Siberian Squill is an early-blooming, six-petal flower in the lily family. This block is so flowerlike in appearance that I was pleased to find an unusual flower name to attach to it.

Shape	Number per Block
P	6 (3 *each* of 2 fabrics)
D	6 light

Block Size	Patterns to Use
3"	P2, D1
6"	P4, D2

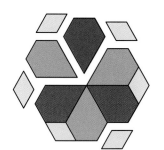
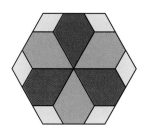

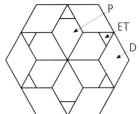

Stargazer

Shape	Number per Block
P	6 (3 *each* of 2 fabrics)
ET	6 dark
D	6 light

Block Size	Patterns to Use
4"	P2, ET1, D2
8"	P4, ET2, D4

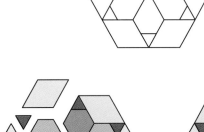
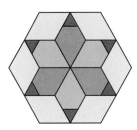

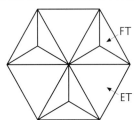

Windmill

Shape	Number per Block
FT	9 (6 light and 3 dark)
ET	3 light

Block Size	Patterns to Use
2"	FT2, ET2
4"	FT4, ET4

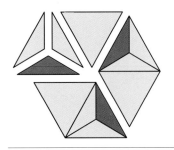
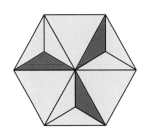

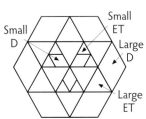

Triad Star

Use the same light and medium-dark fabrics through-out the block.

Shape	Number per Block
Small D	3 medium-dark
Large D	6 light
Small ET	6 medium
Large ET	9 (3 *each* of 3 fabrics: light, medium-dark, and dark)

Block Size	Patterns to Use
4"	D1, ET1, D2, ET2
8"	D2, ET2, D4, ET4

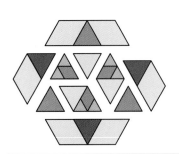
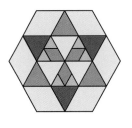

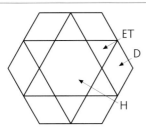

Hexagon Star

Shape	Number per Block
H	1 medium
ET	6 dark
D	6 light (Fabric should sharply contrast with the ET fabric.)

Block Size	Patterns to Use
2"	H1, ET1, D1
4"	H2, ET2, D2
8"	H4, ET4, D4

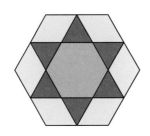

Wagon Wheel

Shape	Number per Block
H	1 light
FHH	6 (3 each of 2 fabrics)

Block Size	Patterns to Use
2"	H1, FHH1
4"	H2, FHH2
8"	H4, FHH4

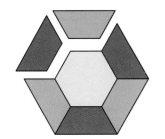
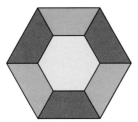

Pirouette

Shape	Number per Block
TK or HK	18 (3 each of 2 fabrics for center hexagon; 12 of contrast for outer ring)

Block Size	Patterns to Use
2"	TK2
3½"	HK2
4"	TK4
7"	HK4

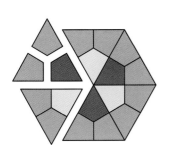
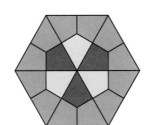

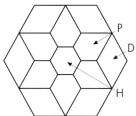

Dolly Madison Star

Shape	Number per Block
H	1 dark
P	6 medium
D	6 light

Block Size	Patterns to Use
4"	H1, P2, D2
8"	H2, P4, D4

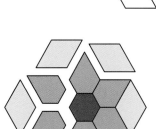
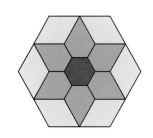

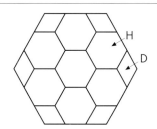

Grandmother's Flower

Shape	Number per Block
H	7 (3 *each* of 2 fabrics; 1 of contrast for center)
D	6 light

Block Size	Patterns to Use
3"	H1, D1
6"	H2, D2
12"	H4, D4

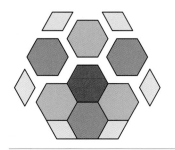
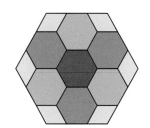

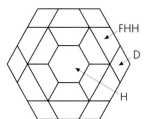

Zinnia

Shape	Number per Block
H	1 dark
FHH	12 (6 *each* of 2 fabrics)
D	6 light

Block Size	Patterns to Use
3"	H1, FHH1, D1
6"	H2, FHH2, D2
12"	H4, FHH4, D4

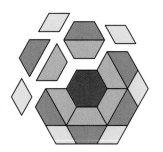
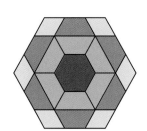

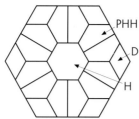

Daisy

Shape	Number per Block
H	1 medium
PHH	12 (6 *each* of 2 fabrics)
D	6 light

Block Size	Patterns to Use
3"	H1, PHH1, D1
6"	H2, PHH2, D2
12"	H4, PHH4, D4

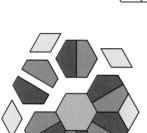 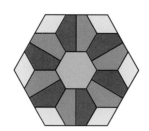

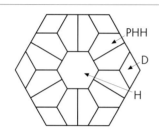 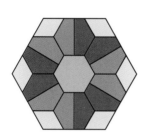

Pansy

The Pansy block is constructed like the Daisy block above. Its different appearance is created by a simple shift in value placement.

Shape	Number per Block
H	1 medium
PHH	12 (6 *each* of 2 fabrics)
D	6 light

Block Size	Patterns to Use
3"	H1, PHH1, D1
6"	H2, PHH2, D2
12"	H4, PHH4, D4

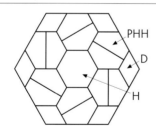

Waterwheel

The components of the Waterwheel block are the same as the Pansy and Daisy blocks above. The difference comes with value or color placement and a twist of the Night and Day Hexagon units.

Shape	Number per Block
H	1 medium
PHH	12 (3 *each* of 2 fabrics; 6 light)
D	6 light

Block Size	Patterns to Use
3"	H1, PHH1, D1
6"	H2, PHH2, D2
12"	H4, PHH4, D4

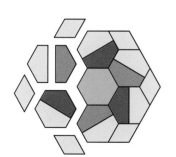 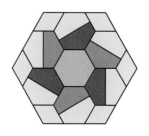

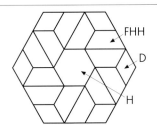

Ferris Wheel

Shape	Number per Block
H	1 medium
FHH	12 (6 *each* of dark and light)
D	6 light

Block Size	Patterns to Use
3"	H1, FHH1, D1
6"	H2, FHH2, D2
12"	H4, FHH4, D4

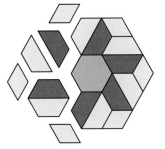
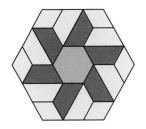

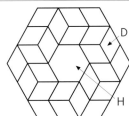

Quantum Spin

Shape	Number per Block
H	1 dark
D	24 (6 medium; 6 medium-dark; 12 light)

Block Size	Patterns to Use
3"	H1, D1
6"	H2, D2
12"	H4, D4

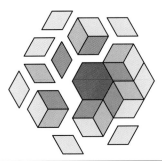
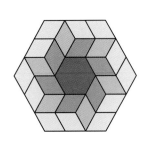

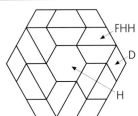

Propeller

Shape	Number per Block
H	1 medium
FHH	12 (3 medium; 3 dark; 6 light)
D	6 (3 *each* of dark and light)

Block Size	Patterns to Use
3"	H1, FHH1, D1
6"	H2, FHH2, D2
12"	H4, FHH4, D4

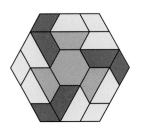

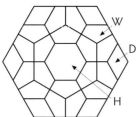

Tasmanian Devil

Shape	Number per Block
H	1 medium-light
W	18 (6 *each* of medium, dark, and light)
D	6 light

Block Size	Patterns to Use
3"	H1, W1, D1
6"	H2, W2, D2
12"	H4, W4, D4

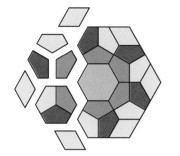
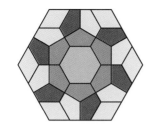

Shooting Star

Use the same fabric for all of the pieces except the star points or, for a different look, cut the central hexagon from the fabric used for the star points.

Shape	Number per Block
H	1 light
HK	6 light
HD	12 (6 *each* of light and contrast)
D	6 light

Block Size	Patterns to Use
3"	H1, HK2, HD1, D1
6"	H2, HK4, HD2, D2

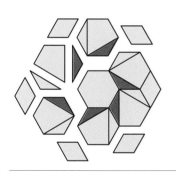
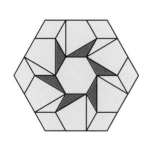

Comet

Shape	Number per Block
H	1 light
HD	12 (6 *each* of medium and dark)
HK	6 light
D	6 light

Block Size	Patterns to Use
3"	H1, HK2, HD1, D1
6"	H2, HK4, HD2, D2

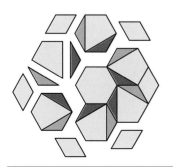
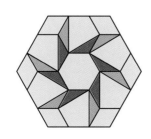

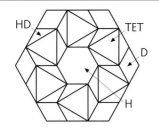

Vortex

Shape	Number per Block
H	1 light
HD	18 dark
TET	6 medium
D	6 light

Block Size	Patterns to Use
3"	H1, HD1, TET1, D1
6"	H2, HD2, TET2, D2
12"	H4, HD4, TET4, D4

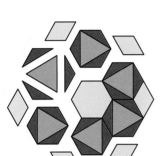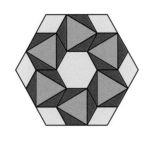

Hex in a Hex

Shape	Number per Block
H	1 light
W	6 dark
HET	12 medium (Cut 6 regular and 6 reversed; see page 20.)

Block Size	Patterns to Use
2"	H1, W1, HET1
4"	H2, W2, HET2
8"	H4, W4, HET4

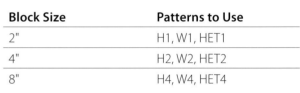

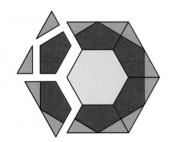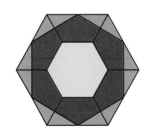

Radiant Hexagon

Shape	Number per Block
H	1 dark
FT	6 light
TK	12 (Use a third fabric or match the hexagon fabric.)

Block Size	Patterns to Use
4"	H2, FT2, TK4

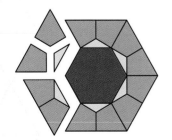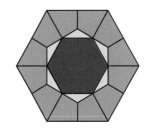

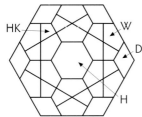

Dreamcatcher

Shape	Number per Block
H	1 light
W	12 (6 *each* of 2 medium fabrics)
HK	12 dark
D	6 light

Block Size	Patterns to Use
6"	H2, W2, HK2, D2
12"	H4, W4, HK4, D4

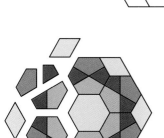
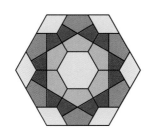
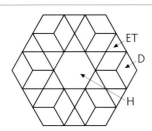

Blooming Star

Shape	Number per Block
H	1 medium
ET	12 (6 medium; 6 light)
D	18 (12 dark; 6 light)

Block Size	Patterns to Use
3"	H1, ET1, D1
6"	H2, ET2, D2
12"	H4, ET4, D4

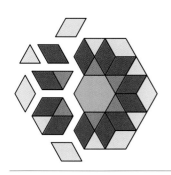
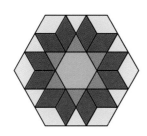

Brilliant Star

Shape	Number per Block
D	6 (3 *each* of 2 fabrics)
H	6 light
ET	6 dark

Block Size	Patterns to Use
3"	D1, H1, ET1
6"	D2, H2, ET2
12"	D4, H4, ET4

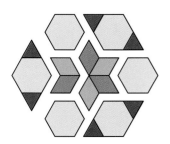
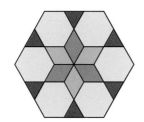

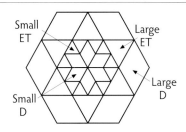

Star in a Star

Shape	Number per Block
Small D	6 medium-light (6 matching *or* 3 *each* of 2 fabrics)
Large D	6 dark
Small ET	12 medium-dark
Large ET	6 light

Block Size	Patterns to Use
4"	D1, ET1, D2, ET2
8"	D2, ET2, D4, ET4

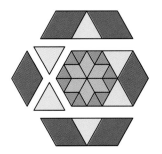
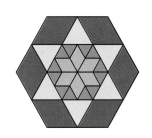

Shimmering Star

Shape	Number per Block
D	18 (6 medium for center star; 12 dark for Argyle Hexagon units)
ET	18 (6 medium; 12 light for Argyle Hexagon units)

Block Size	Patterns to Use
3"	D1, ET1
6"	D2, ET2
12"	D4, ET4

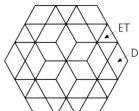

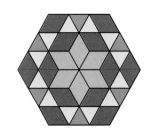

Starflower

Shape	Number per Block
H	1 dark
P	6 medium
D	12 (6 *each* of light and medium-light)
ET	18 (12 dark; 6 light)

Block Size	Patterns to Use
6"	H1, P2, D2, ET2
12"	H2, P4, D4, ET4

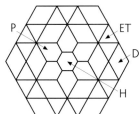
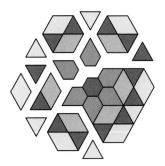
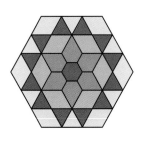

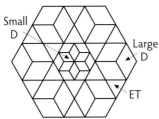

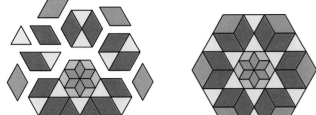

Rising Star

Shape	Number per Block
Small D	12 (6 *each* of medium and medium-light)
Large D	18 (12 dark; 6 medium)
ET	12 light

Block Size	Patterns to Use
6"	D1, D2, ET2
12"	D2, D4, ET4

Diamond Blocks ◆

These blocks are full of inspiration for argyle and harlequin designs.

Four-Patch Diamond

Shape	Number per Block
D	4 (2 *each* of light and dark)

Block Size	Patterns to Use
2"	D1
4"	D2
8"	D4

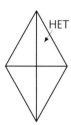 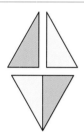 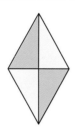

Jester Diamond

Shape	Number per Block
HET	4 (2 *each* of light and dark. Cut 1 regular and 1 reversed; see page 20.)

Block Size	Patterns to Use
2"	HET2
4"	HET4

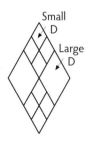  

Diamond Chips

Shape	Number per Block
Small D	8 (4 *each* of medium and dark)
Large D	2 light

Block Size	Patterns to Use
4"	D1, D2
8"	D2, D4

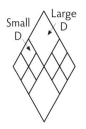
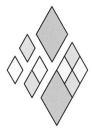

Argyle Diamond

The components and construction of the Argyle Diamond block are exactly the same as the Diamond Chips block on page 52, but the placement of the four-patch units and the larger diamond pieces are switched. As with the Diamond Chips block, choose three fabrics that contrast with each other for the most visually interesting block.

Shape	Number per Block
Small D	8 (4 *each* of light and medium)
Large D	2 dark

Block Size	Patterns to Use
4"	D1, D2
8"	D2, D4

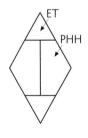
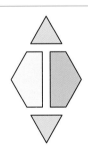
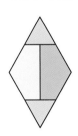

Night and Day Diamond

Shape	Number per Block
ET	2 medium
PHH	2 (1 *each* of light and dark)

Block Size	Patterns to Use
2"	ET1, PHH1
4"	ET2, PHH2
8"	ET4, PHH4

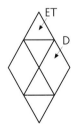

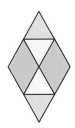

Hourglass Diamond

Shape	Number per Block
ET	4 (2 *each* of light and medium)
D	2 dark

Block Size	Patterns to Use
2"	ET1, D1
4"	ET2, D2
8"	ET4, D4

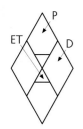  

Sparkling Diamond

Shape	Number per Block
P	2 medium
ET	2 light
D	2 dark

Block Size	Patterns to Use
4"	P2, ET1, D2
8"	P4, ET2, D4

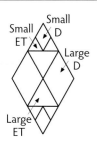 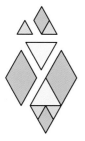 

Shattered Diamond

Shape	Number per Block
Small D	2 dark
Small ET	4 medium
Large D	2 dark
Large ET	2 light (Fabric should sharply contrast with the large-D fabric.)

Block Size	Patterns to Use
4"	D1, ET1, D2, ET2
8"	D2, ET2, D4, ET4

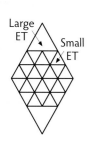  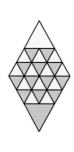

Speckled Diamond

Shape	Number per Block
Small ET	24 (12 *each* of light and dark)
Large ET	2 (1 *each* of the same 2 fabrics as small ET)

Block Size	Patterns to Use
4"	ET1, ET2
8"	ET2, ET4

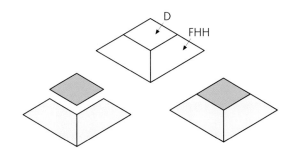

Offset Diamond

Shape	Number per Block
D	1 dark
FHH	2 light

Block Size	Patterns to Use
2"	D1, FHH1
4"	D2, FHH2
8"	D4, FHH4

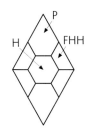 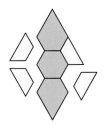 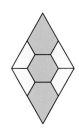

Bow Tie

Shape	Number per Block
H	1 dark
P	2 dark
FHH	4 light

Block Size	Patterns to Use
4"	H1, P2, FHH1
8"	H2, P4, FHH2

Six-Pointed Star Blocks ✶

Any six of the diamond blocks can be joined to create an interesting six-pointed star block. The diamond blocks in this book have finished side lengths of 2", 4", or 8", depending on the shapes used to create them. Those diamonds combine to create star blocks with a finished measurement, from star point to star point, of *approximately* 7", 14", or 28".

To create a six-pointed star from the pieced diamond blocks, set the diamonds together as shown.

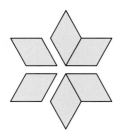 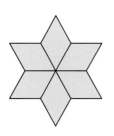

To create a hexagon block, add diamonds or half diamonds between the star points, referring to the tables at right to determine the templates needed. For stars made from 2" diamonds, use the D2 or HD2 patterns; for stars made from 4" diamonds, use D4 or HD4. Stars made from 8" diamonds require a diamond or a half diamond that finishes 8" per side; although there are no patterns of that size in this book, the information needed to draft them can be found in "The 60-Degree Group of Shapes" on page 11. Remember to add seam allowances to any new patterns you draft.

All the dimensions in the tables below are finished sizes, without seam allowances. In addition to the hexagon block's side length, the hexagon width (from a point to its opposite point) and its height (from one side to the opposite side) are given.

Diamond Setting Pieces for Six-Pointed Stars

Star-Diamond Side	Setting Pattern	Hexagon Side	Hexagon Width	Hexagon Height
2"	D2	4"	8"	Scant 7"
4"	D4	8"	16"	Ample 13¾"
8"	Draft a pattern	16"	32"	Scant 27¾"

Half Diamond Setting Pieces for Six-Pointed Stars

Star-Diamond Side	Setting Pattern	Hexagon Side	Hexagon Width	Hexagon Height
2"	HD2	Scant 3½"	Scant 7"	Scant 6"
4"	HD4	Scant 7"	Scant 13⅞"	Scant 12"
8"	Draft a pattern	Scant 13⅞"	Scant 27¾"	Scant 24"

If you don't wish to make the stars into hexagon blocks, the stars can simply be set together using diamonds or hexagons as shown in "Setting Options" on page 62.

Following are diagrams of stars made from the pieced diamond blocks in this book:

Protostar. Made from six Four-Patch Diamond blocks with original value placement; see page 52.

Neutron Star. Made from six Four-Patch Diamond blocks with alternative value placement.

Nebula. Made from six Four-Patch Diamond blocks, using three blocks each of two value arrangements.

Fractured Star. Made from six Jester Diamond blocks; see page 52.

Quasar. Made from six Diamond Chips blocks; see page 52.

Aurora. Made from six Argyle Diamond blocks; see page 53.

Cosmic Eclipse. Made from six Night and Day Diamond blocks; see page 53.

Big Bang. Made from six Hourglass Diamond blocks; see page 53.

Black Hole. Made from six Sparkling Diamond blocks; see page 54. Note the illusion of a circle lying beneath the chevron points.

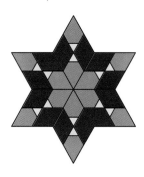

Binary Star. Made from six Shattered Diamond blocks; see page 54.

Convergence Star. Made from six Speckled Diamond blocks; see page 54.

Speckled Star. Leaving off the dark triangle at one point of the Speckled Diamond block creates a Speckled Petal block. Sewing six Speckled Petal blocks to an H2 (for the smaller petal) or H4 (for the larger petal) creates the Speckled Star block. The central hexagon eliminates the bulk at the center of the block where many seams would otherwise converge.

Super Nova. Made from six Offset Diamond blocks; see page 55.

Snowflake. Made from six Bow Tie blocks; see page 55.

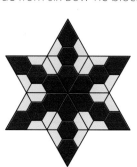

BONUS: Square Six-Pointed Star Block

I thought it would be interesting and versatile to draft a six-pointed star into a square setting. It requires two extra templates, which are found on page 94, and the D2 template on page 90. Begin by cutting strips across the fabric width as detailed below, and then cut out each template shape. The finished block is 7" x 7".

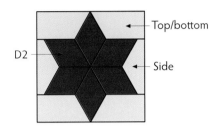

Shape	Number per Block	Fabric Strip Width
D2	6 (all 1 fabric, 3 *each* of 2 fabrics, *or* 1 *each* of 6 fabrics)	2¼"
Side	2	2"
Top/bottom	4 (2 regular and 2 reversed)	2¼"

1. Using Y-seams, piece together the six D2 diamonds to make the central star. Press the seam allowances as desired (see page 26).

2. If you're using multiple fabrics for the diamonds, position the star with the preferred diamond pointing upward. Set in a side section between the two diamond points on each side. Press the seam allowances toward the star.

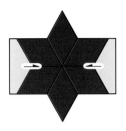

3. Set in the four top/bottom sections. Press the seam allowances toward the background fabric.

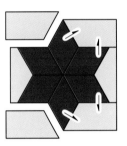

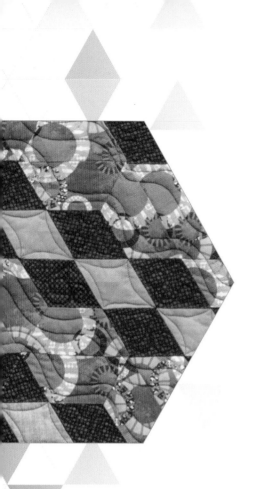

Putting It All Together

Determining the setting for patchwork blocks is one of my favorite parts of quiltmaking. The setting adds tremendous variability and pizzazz to a given set of blocks. As with square quilt blocks, the setting options for hexagons, 60° diamonds, equilateral triangles, and six-pointed stars are varied and practically limitless.

Setting Options

The setting options that I'm going to show you are only the tip of the iceberg, and I hope that they will provide a springboard for you as you begin to explore settings for your 60° family of blocks.

The outer edges of quilts made from any of the 60° group of blocks are not always straight; that is, they're not rectangular like traditional quilts. I have seen many vintage and antique quilts made from these shapes where the quiltmaker used the uneven edges as a design element, finishing the quilt by binding around the irregularly shaped edges. If that's a look you like, it's a perfectly fine option! However, I'll offer some suggestions for employing different shapes around the periphery to achieve straight edges, which allow the option of adding borders to your quilt.

Settings for Hexagon Blocks

Hexagons can easily be set with other hexagons of the same size, resulting in rows of offset hexagons. You may choose to set whole-cloth or pieced hexagons together, or combine the two in an alternating (or random) arrangement.

For straight edges in a quilt top made entirely of hexagons, add flat half hexagons (FHH) in the corresponding size to two opposite edges. Use half diamonds (HD) in the corresponding size to straighten the remaining sides of the quilt, and add half equilateral triangles (HET) at the corners.

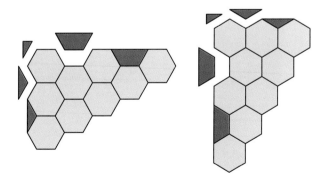

Hexagons can also be set with their corresponding equilateral triangles (ET). In the first illustration, note how the hexagons are straight in rows across, but they are offset from one row to the next. Along the top row, the equilateral triangles set between the hexagons create a straight edge. Along the sides, pointy half hexagons (PHH) and half equilateral triangles (HET) are the fillers that create a straight edge. At each corner, a half equilateral triangle (HET) creates the desired 90° angle.

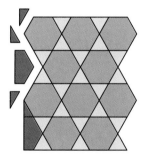

When we place the hexagons "on point," they align in vertical rows to create straight quilt sides, but the hexagons are offset in relation to the next vertical row. Use the same filler pieces as in the previous example, but place them along the top and bottom edges of the quilt.

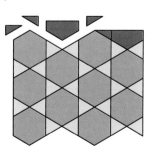

Hexagons can also be set in rows with 60° diamonds (D). The hexagons align both horizontally and vertically, whether oriented with a flat edge or a point at the top. Along the quilt edge with the hexagon sides, an equilateral triangle (ET) becomes the filler to create a straight edge, while set-in half diamonds (HD) fill the gaps between hexagon points. Four half equilateral triangles (HET), two regular and two reversed, straighten the corners to 90°.

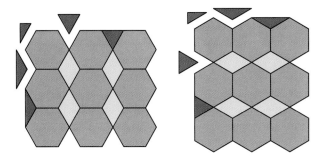

Individual hexagon blocks, either whole-cloth or pieced, can easily be transformed into rectangular blocks by adding half equilateral triangles (HET; two regular and two reversed) to the corners. This opens the way to a variety of setting options using sashing between the blocks.

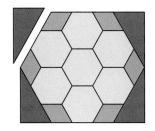

Settings for Equilateral-Triangle Blocks

The most obvious way to piece together equilateral triangles is to arrange them in horizontal rows of same-sized blocks, alternating point-up and point-down placement. The bases of the point-up triangles in the first row align with the bases of the point-down triangles in the row beneath. As with the hexagons, these blocks can be whole-cloth triangles, pieced triangles, or a combination of the two.

With triangles aligned this way, straight edges are automatically created at the top and bottom edges of the quilt top. To create straight side edges, either regular and reversed half equilateral triangles (HET) or half diamonds (HD) in sizes that correspond with the equilateral triangle can be used as fillers.

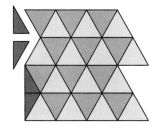 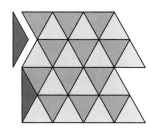

Triangles in horizontal rows can also be off set, with the midpoint of a triangle base in the first row aligned with the apex (top point) of a triangle in the row beneath. The top and bottom of the quilt will have straight edges and regular and reversed half equilateral triangles (HET) serve as fillers along the side edges. As you can see, varying the value placement creates two very different looks in the quilt top.

Setting pieced triangles with hexagons or diamonds is also very effective visually. The large, whole-cloth pieces provide wonderful open spaces for beautiful quilting.

Settings for Diamond Blocks

Diamond blocks may be oriented horizontally or vertically. As with the previously discussed shapes, diamonds, whether whole-cloth, pieced, or a mixture, can be set side by side to create a quilt top. Use equilateral triangles (ET), half diamonds (HD), and both regular and reversed half equilateral triangles (HET) to form straight edges and 90° corners.

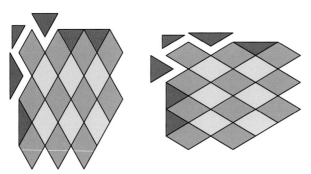

As always, value placement plays a very effective role in the outcome of the quilt. Experiment with different values and placement options as you plan the quilt layout.

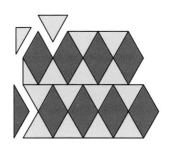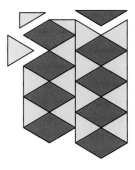

Another visually interesting, fun, and simple way to set diamonds is to create chevrons. Begin by piecing the diamonds in strips, making a left-leaning strip and a right-leaning strip. Press the seam allowances of the left-leaning strip toward the bottom of the strip, and press the seam allowances of the right-leaning strip upward. Place the strips right sides together, matching the seam lines, and stitch the central seam. The pressing ensures that the angled seams nestle together happily as you sew, creating perfect seam alignment at each chevron point. Press the central seam allowance to one side.

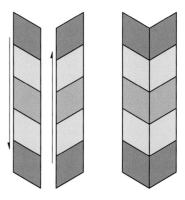

Chevron strips can be joined directly or with sashing between them. Straighten the upper and lower edges and corners with half diamonds (HD) and regular and reversed half equilateral triangles (HET).

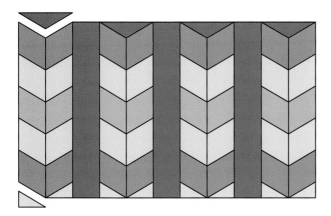

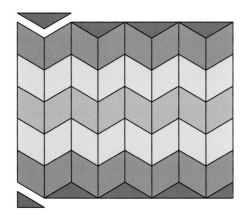

Settings for Six-Pointed Star Blocks

We've already explored the use of diamonds and half diamonds as setting pieces with six-pointed stars, creating hexagon blocks. However, it's not necessary to convert the star into a hexagon before setting it into a quilt top.

Six-pointed stars can be set with 60° diamonds between them. This setting creates overlapping horizontal rows of stars that are offset from one row to the next.

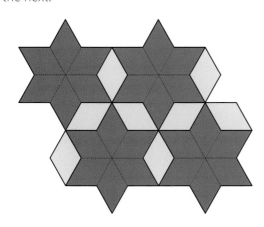

Six-pointed stars can also be set in horizontal and vertical rows without overlaps and offsets. One way to achieve this is to set the stars in horizontal rows with a single 60° diamond between pairs of stars. Align the rows so that the stars meet vertically, point to point. The gap created at the center of four stars can be filled with five 60° diamonds set together as shown. If the center diamond contrasts in color or value with the other four diamonds, it creates a secondary design across the quilt top.

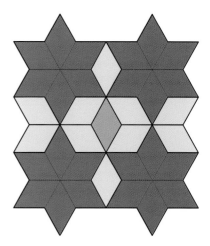

Another interesting secondary design is created by setting horizontal and vertical rows of six-pointed stars with a combination of hexagons and equilateral triangles.

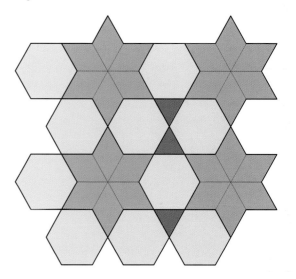

There are many, many setting options available as you play with the 60° family of shapes. I hope that these examples have provided inspiration for you as you continue to explore more and more possibilities!

Calculating Shape Dimensions

All quiltmaking requires some math, so most quilters are familiar with certain fractions and their decimal equivalents. When determining the size and shape of patterns derived from hexagons, your calculations often lead to a number that extends three or more places beyond the decimal point. Like all quilters, you round up or down to the closest ⅛", using these decimal equivalents for fractions:

⅛ = 0.125	⅝ = 0.625
¼ = 0.25	¾ = 0.75
⅜ = 0.375	⅞ = 0.875
½ = 0.5	

Keep these facts in mind as you work with the hexagon-derived shapes in this book and calculate dimensions for your own blocks and quilts.

▶ The lengths of all six sides of a regular hexagon are equal.

▶ The distance from the center point of a regular hexagon to any of its outer corners is equal to its side length.

▶ The distance from one corner of a regular hexagon to its opposite corner is twice the length of one side.

▶ The distance from one corner of a regular hexagon to its opposite corner is *longer* than the distance from one side of the same hexagon to its opposite side.

▶ All three sides of an equilateral triangle are equal in length.

▶ The distance from one corner of an equilateral triangle to the center point of the opposite side is *shorter* than the side length of the same triangle.

▶ All four sides of a 60° diamond are equal to one another.

▶ A 60° diamond can be made by placing two equilateral triangles together, base to base.

There are detailed geometric equations that can be used to determine the dimensions of the hexagon, equilateral triangle, and 60° diamond. Thankfully, you don't need to know them, but there's one number to memorize: 86.6%.

Hexagon Dimensions

The distance from one side of a hexagon to the opposite side is 86.6% of the distance from one corner of a hexagon to the opposite corner.

Example 1: The finished side length of a hexagon is 4". What are the height and width of that hexagon? The finished distance between opposite corners of the hexagon is twice the side length, so the hexagon's corner-to-corner width is 8". The distance between two parallel sides (side-to-side height) is calculated in the following way:

8" x 86.6% (or 0.866) = 6.928, which is rounded up to 7"

Example 2: What are the dimensions of a hexagon with a finished side length of 3½"?

3.5" x 2 = 7" (corner-to-corner width)

7" x 0.866 = 6.062", which is rounded down to 6" (side-to-side height)

Finished Measurements of Hexagons

Side Length	Corner-to-Corner (Width)	Side-to-Side (Height)	Height Rounded to Nearest ⅛"
1"	2"	1.73"	1¾"
2"	4"	3.464"	3½"
3"	6"	5.196"	5¼"
4"	8"	6.928"	7"
6"	12"	10.392"	10⅜"
8"	16"	13.856"	13⅞"
12"	24"	20.78"	20¾"

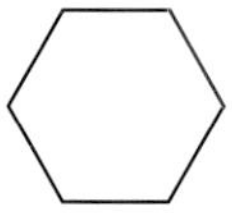

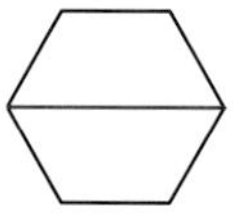

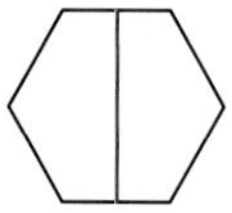

Equilateral-Triangle Dimensions

All three sides of an equilateral triangle are the same length. To calculate the triangle's height, or the distance from the apex (point) of the triangle to the midpoint of the base, multiply the side length by 86.6%.

Example 1: What is the height of an equilateral triangle with a finished side length of 4"?

4" x 0.866 = 3.464", which is rounded up to 3½"

Example 2: What is the height of an equilateral triangle with a finished side length of 3"?

3" x 0.866 = 2.598", which is rounded up to 2⅝"

Finished Measurements of Equilateral Triangles

Side Length	Height	Height Rounded to Nearest ⅛"
1"	0.866"	⅞"
2"	1.732"	1¾"
3"	2.598"	2⅝"
3½"	3.031"	3"
4"	3.464"	3½"
6"	5.196"	5¼"
7"	6.062"	6"
8"	6.928"	7"
12"	10.392"	10⅜"

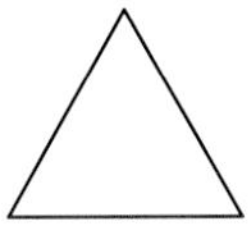

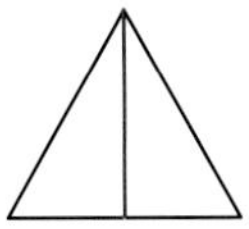

60-Degree Diamond Dimensions

If you'll recall, a 60° diamond can be divided into two equilateral triangles, so the diamond's width is equal to the length of one side. Calculating the longest measurement of the diamond (from one narrow point to the other), begins with finding the height of one of the triangles by multiplying the side length by 86.6%. The answer is half the height of the diamond, so multiplying it by two provides the height of the diamond.

Example 1: What is the height of a 60° diamond with a finished side length of 4"?

4" x 0.866 = 3.464"

3.464" x 2 = 6.928", which is rounded up to 7"

Example 2: What is the height of a 60° diamond with a finished side length of 6"?

6" x 0.866 = 5.192"

5.192" x 2 = 10.384", which is rounded down to 10⅜"

Finished Measurements of 60-Degree Diamonds

Side Length	Width	Height	Height Rounded to Nearest ⅛"
1"	1"	1.732"	1¾"
2"	2"	3.464"	3½"
3½"	3½"	6.062"	6"
4"	4"	6.928"	7"
6"	6"	10.392"	10⅜"
7"	7"	12.124"	12⅛"
8"	8"	13.856"	13⅞"

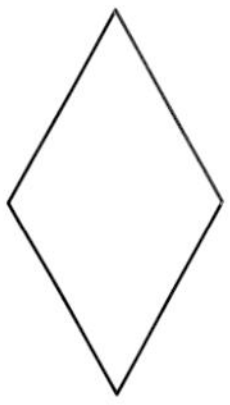

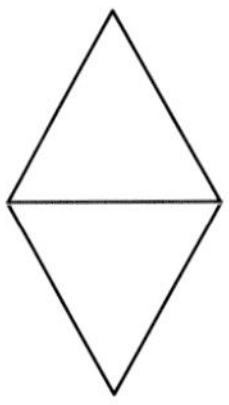

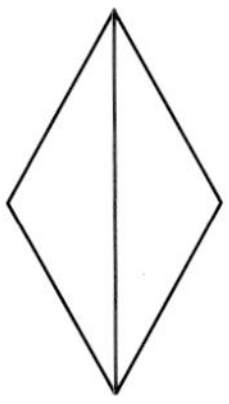

Fiesta Table Topper

This festive table topper is quick and fun to piece, making it the perfect introduction to working with Y-seams.

Materials

Yardage is based on 42"-wide fabric.

⅔ yard of large-scale yellow print for border and binding

⅓ yard of red print for blocks

¼ yard of blue stripe for blocks

¼ yard of yellow print for blocks

⅛ yard of blue print for blocks

⅛ yard of green print for setting diamonds

1 yard of fabric for backing

33" x 36" piece of batting

Cutting

Patterns begin on page 86.

Make plastic templates for pieces D4, ET2, FHH2, and H2. If you are using Small Hexagons Plus, template set G, see page 21.

From the red print, cut:

1 strip, 4" x 42"; cut into 3 hexagons, H2

2 strips, 2¼" x 42"; cut into 18 flat half hexagons, FHH2

From the yellow print, cut:

2 strips, 2¼" x 42"; cut into 24 equilateral triangles, ET2

From the blue print, cut:

1 strip, 2¼" x 42"; cut into 6 flat half hexagons, FHH2

From the blue stripe, cut:

2 strips, 2¼" x 42"; cut into 18 flat half hexagons, FHH2

Pay attention to the direction of the stripes as you cut the pieces.

From the green print, cut:

1 strip, 4" x 42"; cut into 6 diamonds, D4

From the large-scale yellow print, cut:

3 strips, 4" x 42"; crosscut into 6 strips, 4" x 18"

4 strips, 2¼" x 42"

Block Construction

"Fiesta Table Topper" is composed of two different hexagon blocks: Spinner (page 39) and Wagon Wheel (page 43).

Spinner Block

Following the instructions for the individual blocks, make four Spinner blocks, three red and one blue. Use six red flat half hexagons and six yellow equilateral triangles for each red block. For the blue block, use six blue-print flat half hexagons and six yellow equilateral triangles.

Make 3.   Make 1.

The blue Spinner block is set so that it's spinning in the opposite direction than the red Spinner blocks. Follow the illustrations closely for the correct orientation of each triangle unit when you assemble them to make the hexagon blocks.

Wagon Wheel Block

Make three Wagon Wheel blocks, using six blue-striped flat half hexagons and one red hexagon for each.

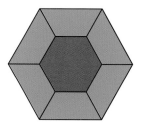

Make 3.

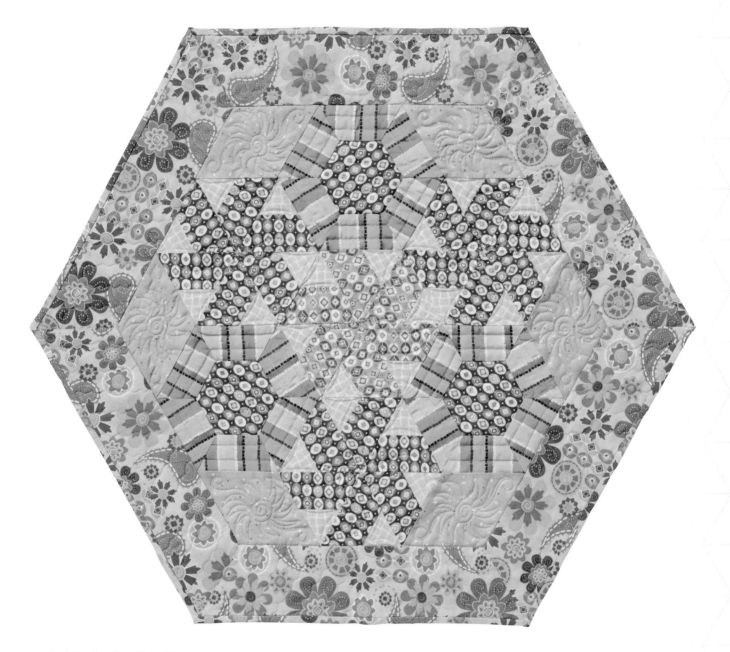

Finished quilt: 29" x 32"

Finished block: 7" x 8"

*"Fiesta Table Topper," machine pieced
and machine quilted by Kelly Ashton*

Quilt-Top Assembly

1. Use Y-seams to join the blocks and setting diamonds as shown. Each unfinished edge should measure 12½" from corner to corner; if not, make a record of the actual edge measurement to use when sizing the border strips.

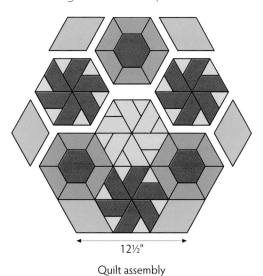

12½"

Quilt assembly

2. To trim each 4" x 18" border strip as shown, begin by using a ruler with a 60° reference line to mark and cut a line from the lower-left corner to the top edge of the strip. Measure 12½" from the top-left corner of the strip along the upper edge and mark the point with a pin. Use the 60° angle line on the ruler to cut from this point to the bottom edge of the strip. *If the unfinished edges of your top measure other than 12½", use your measurement as a guide for cutting the border strips.*

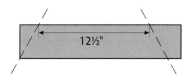

12½"

3. Using Y-seams, sew the border pieces to the edges of the quilt top and to each other. Press the seam allowances toward the border.

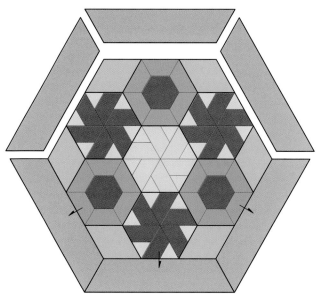

Adding borders

Completing the Table Topper

For more information on finishing techniques, go to ShopMartingale.com/HowtoQuilt for free, illustrated instructions.

1. Sandwich the quilt top, batting, and backing fabric. Quilt as desired.

2. Trim the batting and backing to match the quilt top.

3. Bind the quilt using the yellow 2¼"-wide strips. Enjoy!

Liberty Table Runner

I really love Americana. This patriotic runner is a perfect table adornment for Independence Day, Memorial Day, and Labor Day gatherings, or for any day of the year.

Materials

Yardage is based on 42"-wide fabric.

1⅛ yards of cream print for blocks and binding

⅓ yard of red tone-on-tone for blocks

⅓ yard of dark-blue print for blocks

¼ yard of dark-red print for blocks

⅛ yard of medium-blue print for blocks

1⅓ yards of fabric for backing

26" x 48" piece of batting

Cutting

Patterns begin on page 86.

Make plastic templates for pieces D4, D2, ET4, ET2, FHH2, HD4, and HET4. If you are using Small Hexagons Plus, template set G, see page 21.

From the medium-blue print, cut:

1 strip, 2¼" x 42"; cut into 6 diamonds, D2

From the cream print, cut:

6 strips, 2¼" x 42"; cut into 12 equilateral triangles, ET2, and 66 diamonds, D2

2 strips, 2⅝" x 42"; cut into 10 half diamonds, HD4

2 strips, 4" x 42". Cut into 4 equilateral triangles, ET4; 4 diamonds, D4; 2 half equilateral triangles and 2 half equilateral triangles *reversed*, HET4.

4 strips, 2¼" x 42"

From the red tone-on-tone, cut:

4 strips, 2¼" x 42"; cut into 24 flat half hexagons, FHH2, and 24 equilateral triangles, ET2

From the dark-blue print, cut:

4 strips, 2¼" x 42"; cut into 24 flat half hexagons, FHH2, and 24 equilateral triangles, ET2

From the dark-red print, cut:

2 strips, 2¼" x 42"; cut into 18 diamonds, D2

Faster Folded

It's easy to cut regular and reversed half equilateral triangles at the same time by folding the fabric strip with wrong sides together.

Block Construction

"Liberty Table Runner" is composed of three different hexagon blocks: Dash (page 38), Zigzag (page 38), and Six-Pointed Star (page 41), plus a pieced Half Dash unit (page 73).

Dash Block

Make two Dash blocks, each using two medium-blue D2 diamonds, two cream D4 diamonds, and four cream ET2 equilateral triangles

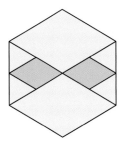

Make 2.

Zigzag Block

Make 12 Zigzag blocks, each using two red FHH2 flat half hexagons, two dark-blue FHH2 flat half hexagons, four cream D2 diamonds, two red ET2 equilateral triangles, and two dark-blue ET2 equilateral triangles.

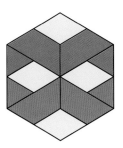

Make 12.

Finished quilt: 20" x 42"
Finished block: 7" x 8"

*"Liberty Table Runner," machine
pieced and machine quilted
by Kelly Ashton*

Six-Pointed Star Block

Make three Six-Pointed Star blocks, each using six dark-red D2 diamonds and six cream D2 diamonds.

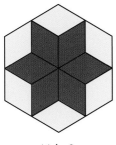

Make 3.

Half Dash Setting Unit

Make two Half Dash setting units, each using one medium-blue D2 diamond, two cream ET2 equilateral triangles, and two cream ET4 equilateral triangles.

1. Make one Diamond Triangle block (see page 30). Press the seam allowances toward the triangles.

2. Sew ET4 triangles to two adjacent sides of the pieced triangle unit as shown. Press the seam allowances toward the larger triangles.

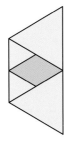

Make 2.

Table-Runner Assembly

1. Using the illustration as a guide, use Y-seams to sew the hexagon blocks together in rows, adding the Half Dash setting units at the ends of the center row. Press the seam allowances within each row in one direction, alternating the direction from row to row.

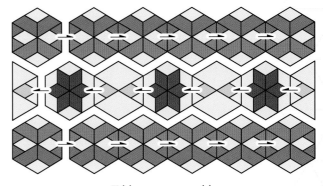

Table-runner assembly

2. Join the rows to make the runner top. Set in the half diamonds and half equilateral triangles to straighten the long edges and corners. Press the seam allowances away from the Zigzag blocks.

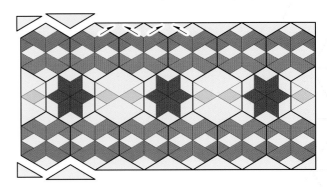

Adding edge and corner pieces

Completing the Table Runner

For more information on finishing techniques, go to ShopMartingale.com/HowtoQuilt for free, illustrated instructions.

1. Sandwich the runner top, batting, and backing fabric. Quilt as desired.

2. Trim the batting and backing to match the runner top.

3. Bind the quilt using the cream 2¼"-wide strips. Enjoy!

Gallery

Painted Mountains, 72" x 76½": Designed and machine pieced by Kelly Ashton; machine quilted by Jeanne Zyck, 2013.

Two-Color Fair Isle, *52" x 73¼": Designed by Kelly Ashton; machine pieced by Susan Thorup; machine quilted by Kelly Ashton, 2013.*

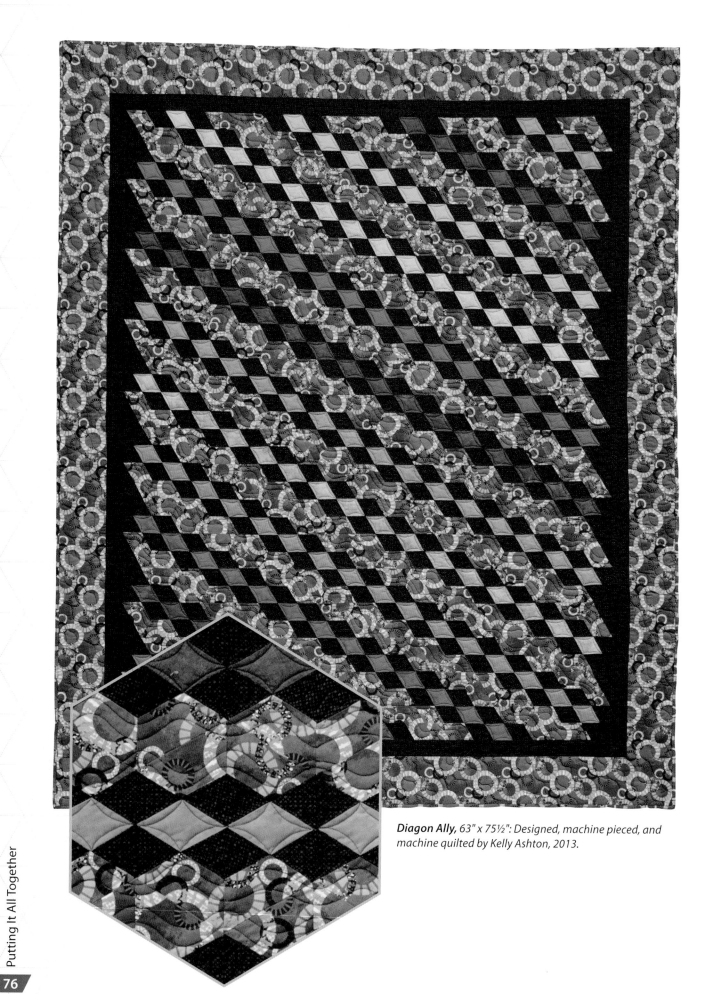

Diagon Ally, *63" x 75½": Designed, machine pieced, and machine quilted by Kelly Ashton, 2013.*

Constellation, *53½" x 67": Designed by Kelly Ashton; machine pieced by Barbara Fife; machine quilted by Jeanne Zyck, 2013.*

Odyssey, *24" x 52": Blocks and setting designed by Kelly Ashton; appliqué design, hand appliqué, and hand quilting by Kathy Delaney; machine quilted by Kelly Ashton, 2013.*

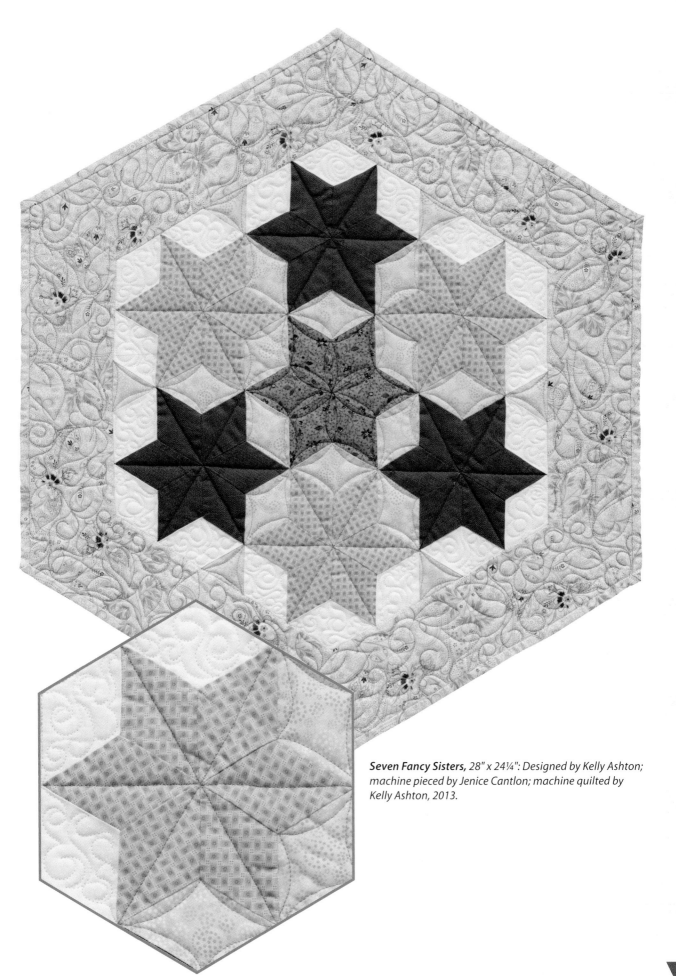

Seven Fancy Sisters, *28" x 24¼": Designed by Kelly Ashton;*
machine pieced by Jenice Cantlon; machine quilted by
Kelly Ashton, 2013.

Days of Old, 34" x 47½": *Designed, machine pieced, and machine quilted by Kelly Ashton, 2013.*

Ring Around the Hexie, *54" x 69½": Designed and machine pieced by Kelly Ashton; machine quilted by Jeanne Zyck, 2013.*

Uncle Johnny's Funky Bow Ties, *65½" x 78": Designed by Kelly Ashton; machine pieced by Jeanne Poore; machine quilted by Jeanne Zyck, 2013.*

Mamo's Flower Garden, *48" x 41½": Designed by Kelly Ashton; machine and hand pieced by Donna Lynn Thomas; machine quilted by Theresa Ward, 2013.*

Kansas Wildflowers, *79" x 84½": Designed, machine pieced, and machine quilted by Kelly Ashton, 2007.*

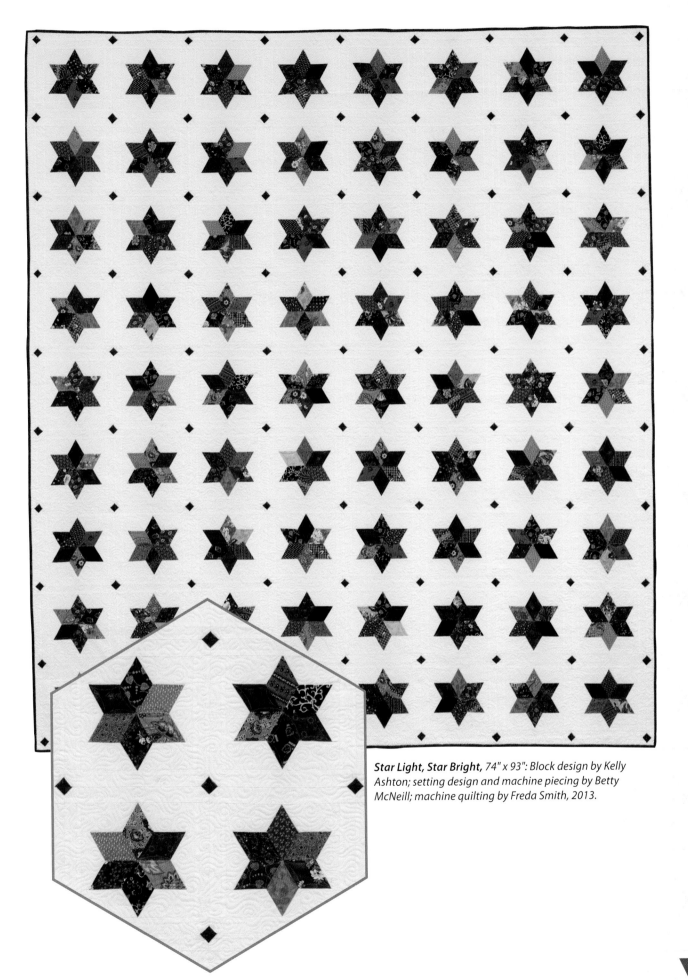

Star Light, Star Bright, 74" x 93": Block design by Kelly Ashton; setting design and machine piecing by Betty McNeill; machine quilting by Freda Smith, 2013.

Patterns

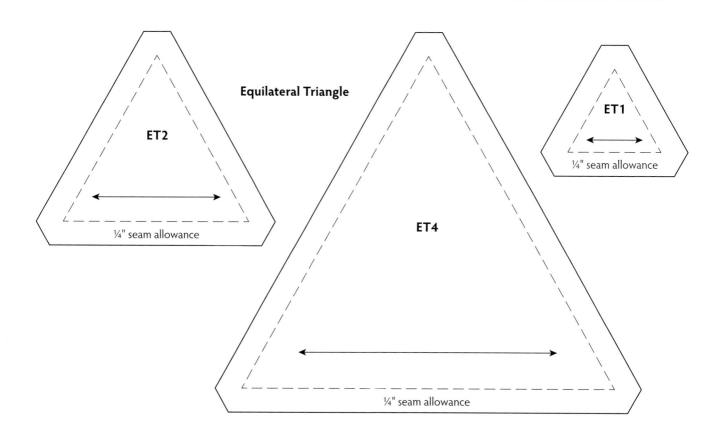

Equilateral Triangle

ET2

ET4

ET1

¼" seam allowance

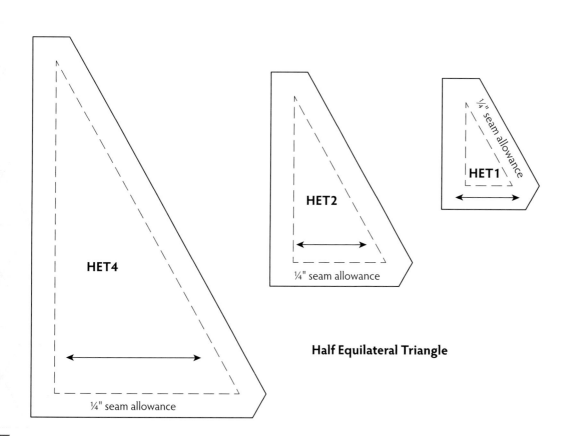

HET4

HET2

HET1

¼" seam allowance

Half Equilateral Triangle

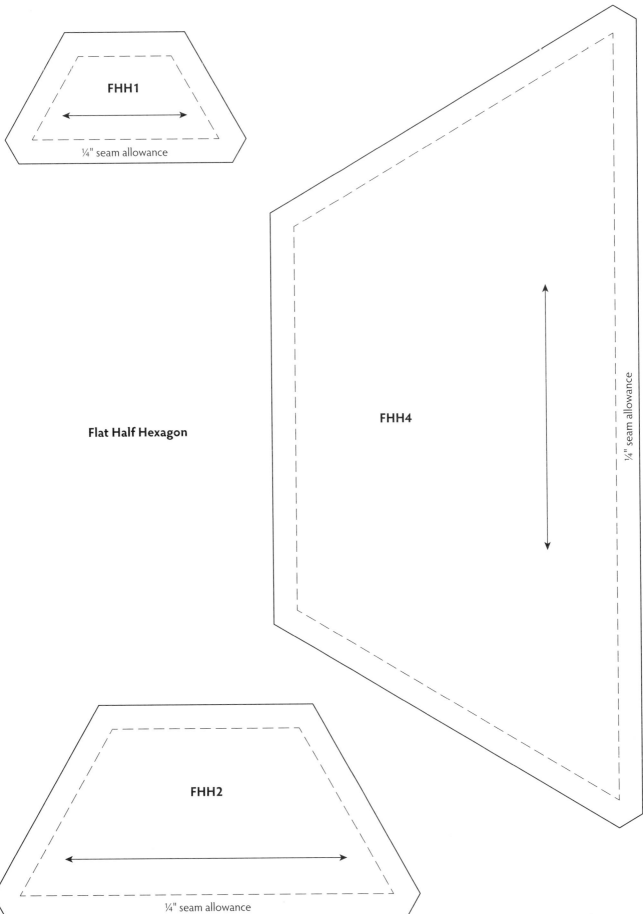

FHH1

¼" seam allowance

Flat Half Hexagon

FHH4

¼" seam allowance

FHH2

¼" seam allowance

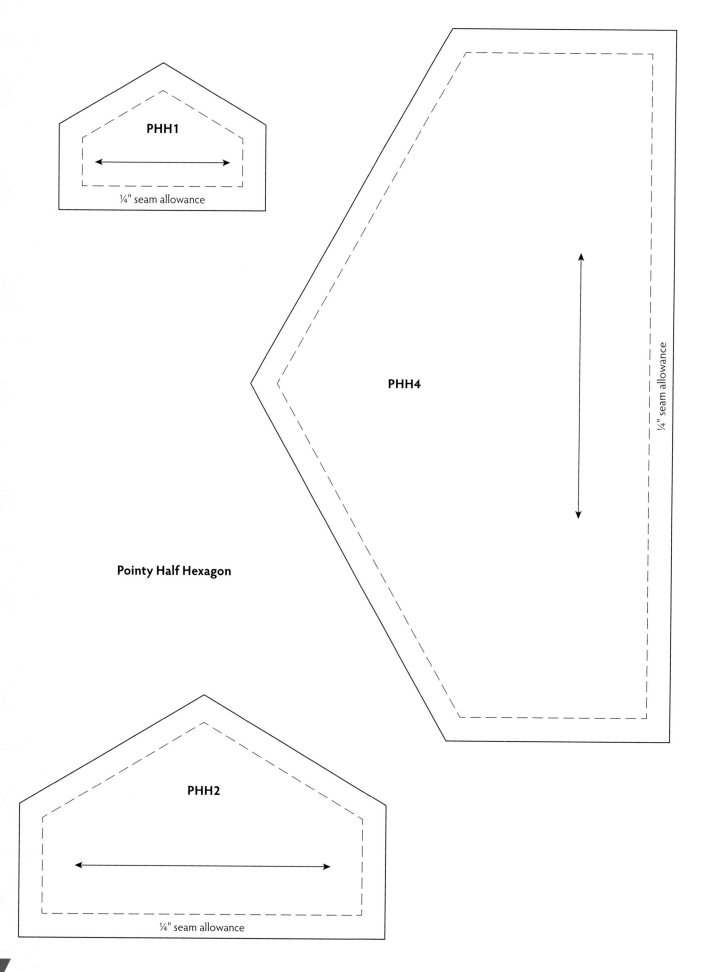

PHH1

¼" seam allowance

PHH4

¼" seam allowance

Pointy Half Hexagon

PHH2

¼" seam allowance

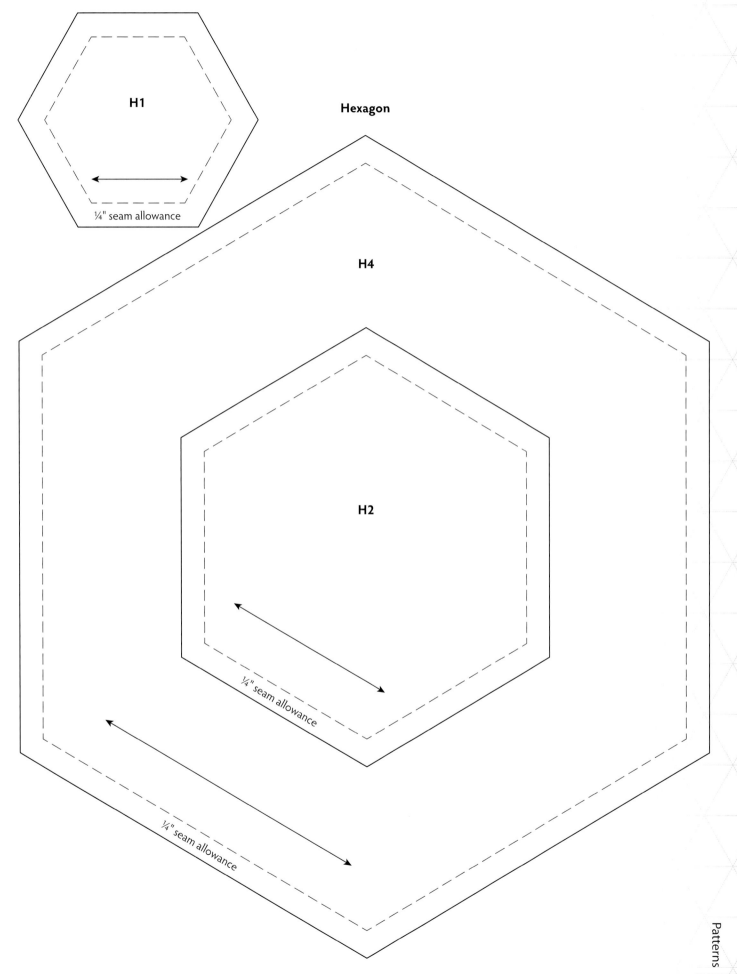

H1

¼" seam allowance

Hexagon

H4

H2

¼" seam allowance

¼" seam allowance

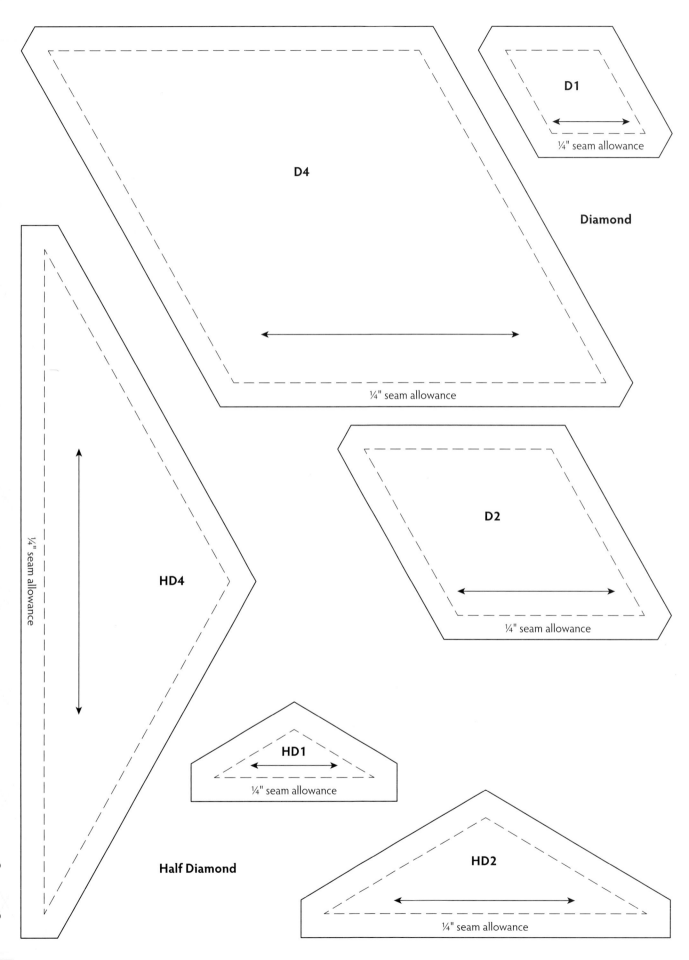

D4

D1

¼" seam allowance

Diamond

¼" seam allowance

¼" seam allowance

D2

¼" seam allowance

HD4

HD1

¼" seam allowance

Half Diamond

HD2

¼" seam allowance

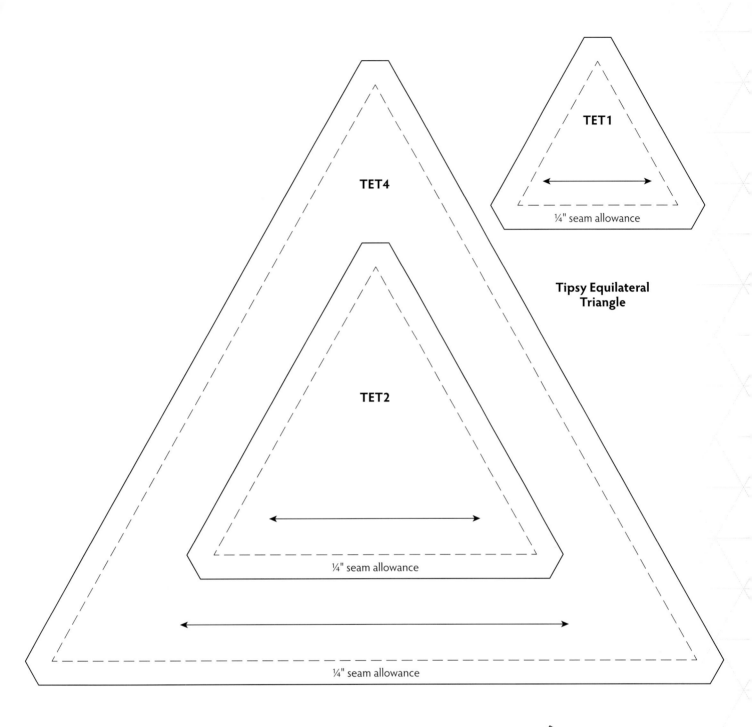

TET4

TET1

¼" seam allowance

Tipsy Equilateral Triangle

TET2

¼" seam allowance

¼" seam allowance

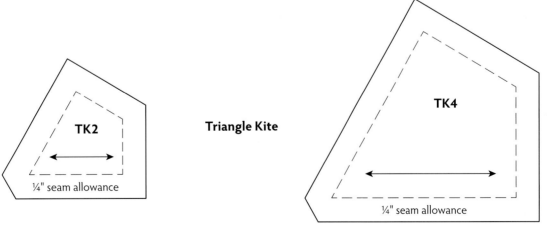

TK2

¼" seam allowance

Triangle Kite

TK4

¼" seam allowance

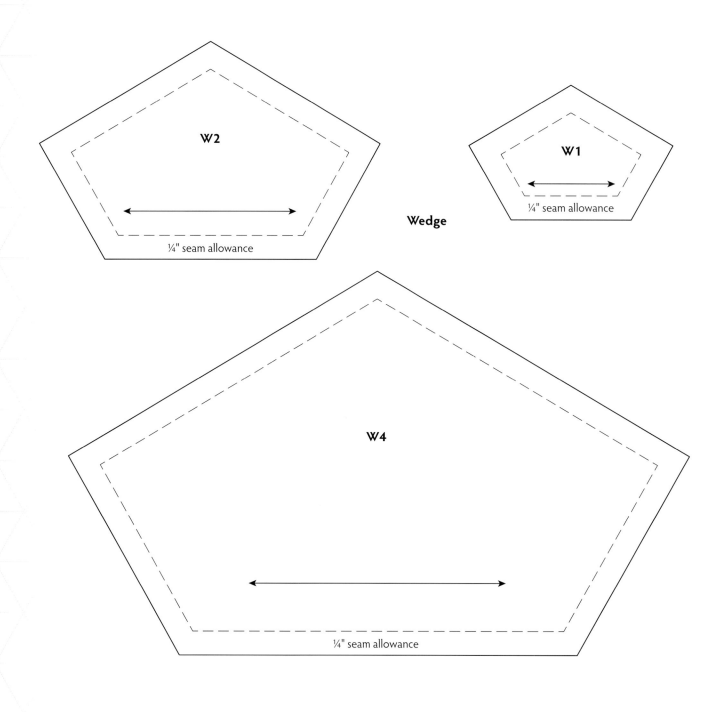

W2

¼" seam allowance

W1

¼" seam allowance

Wedge

W4

¼" seam allowance

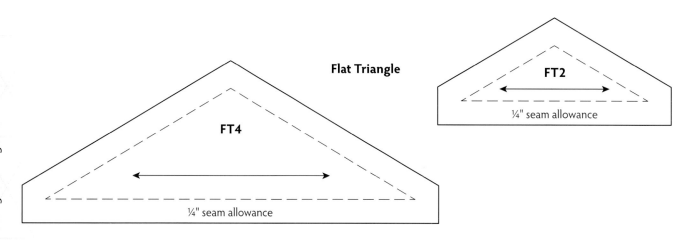

Flat Triangle

FT2

¼" seam allowance

FT4

¼" seam allowance

Hexagon Kite

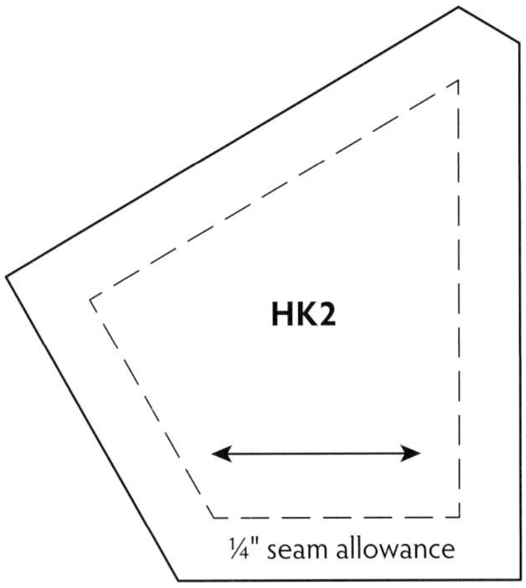

HK2

¼" seam allowance

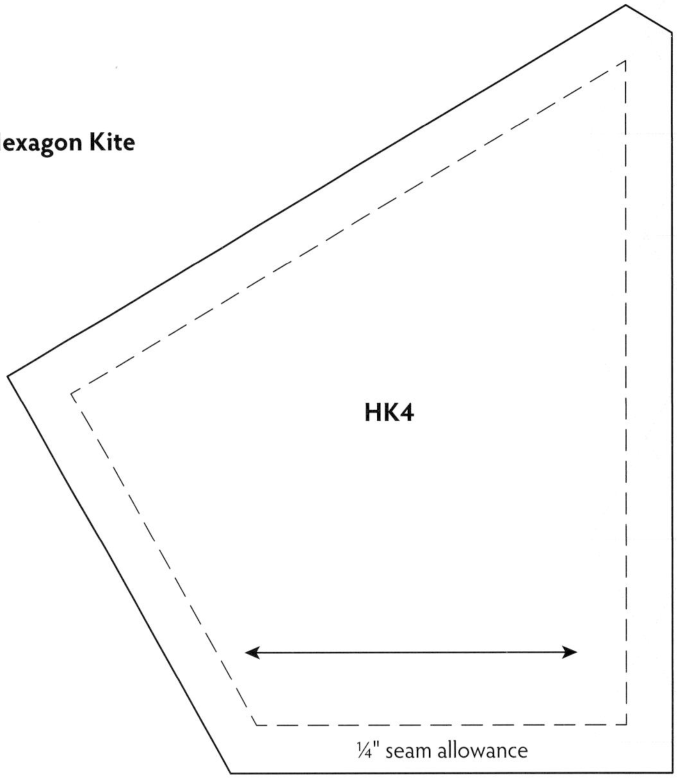

HK4

¼" seam allowance

P4

Petal

P2

¼" seam allowance

¼" seam allowance

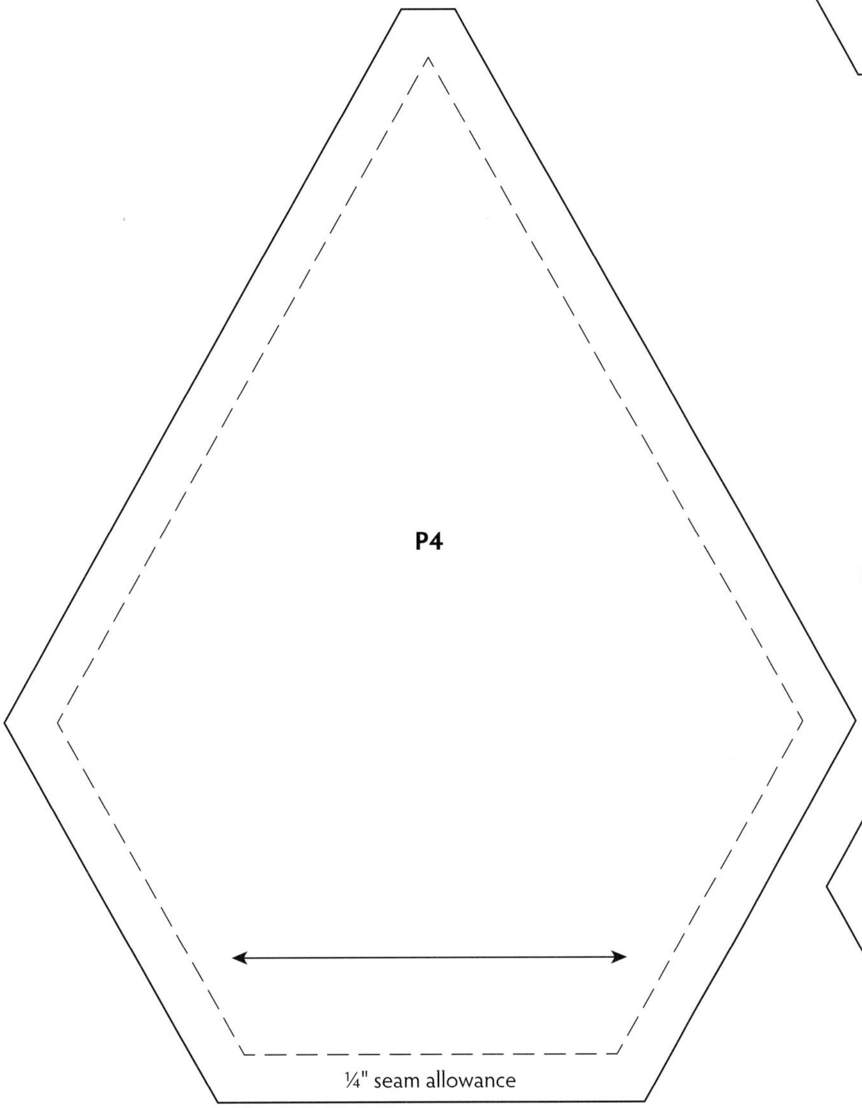

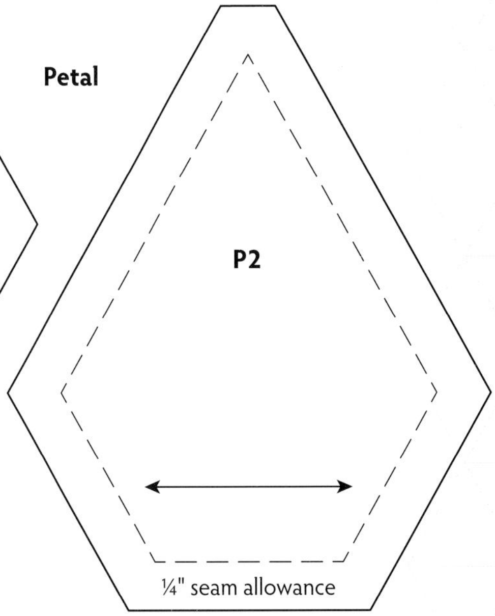

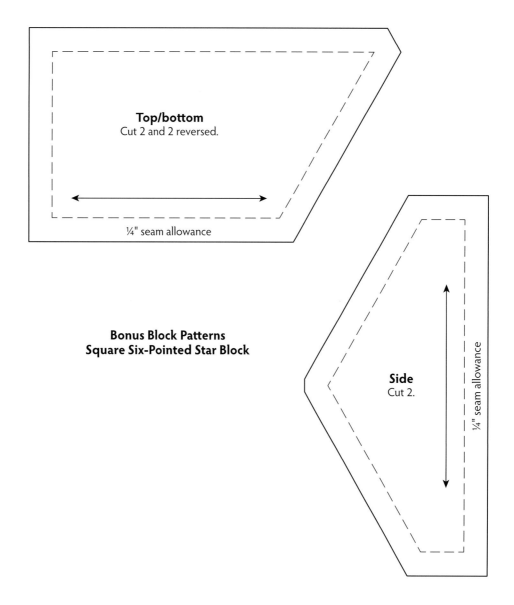

Top/bottom
Cut 2 and 2 reversed.

¼" seam allowance

Bonus Block Patterns
Square Six-Pointed Star Block

Side
Cut 2.

¼" seam allowance

Acknowledgments

With tremendous appreciation and the very clear understanding that creativity cannot occur in a vacuum, I acknowledge:

Everyone at Martingale that I have had the pleasure of encountering, directly or indirectly. All of you have been professional, knowledgeable, and helpful. Thank you! Special thanks to Rebecca Kemp Brent, technical editor, and Tiffany Mottet, copy editor, for asking all the right questions, and then providing suggestions and guidance to ensure accuracy and clarity of information; Christine Erikson, illustrator, for transforming my amateur drawings and photographs into clear representations of the ideas I wished to convey; Brent Kane, photographer, for taking wonderful photographs of the quilts that show both the piecing *and* the quilting; and Connor Chin, cover and interior designer, for the sparkle that your vision and creativity has added to the cover and pages of this book. Creating this book with all of you has been an honor and a privilege!

Marti Michell, who has made tremendous contributions to the world of quiltmaking over the past several decades. I am especially appreciative of her Perfect Patchwork Templates—specifically sets G and H. I'm sure it's no surprise that I love hexagons, equilateral triangles, and 60° diamonds. Though I'm sure I would have eventually made my own way into the 60° family of shapes, I doubt I'd have ventured there when I did if those templates hadn't been available. Thank you, Marti!

Incompetech.com for providing a website that allows us to individualize, download, and print a variety of graph papers, including triangle and hexagon graph papers.

Donna Lynn Thomas, whose pleasant persistence and encouragement propelled me from being an author in my dreams to actually developing and submitting the proposal for this book. Additionally, her mentoring throughout the book-writing process has been invaluable.

My students, from whom I learn so very much—all while having loads of fun!

Carol Kirchhoff, former owner of Prairie Point Quilts in Shawnee, Kansas, for allowing me to create and teach in a wonderful place filled with beautiful fabrics, lovely people, and bountiful inspiration.

Barbara Brackman, a vastly knowledgeable quilt historian who presents that knowledge with flair and humor. Barbara's book, *Encyclopedia of Pieced Quilt Patterns*, allowed me to find names for traditional blocks, and it functioned as a springboard for the creation of new blocks.

I have the good fortune of knowing a lot of truly nice people, and many of them are also talented quiltmakers. It would have been impossible for me to piece, quilt, and bind all of the gallery quilts myself; Jenice Cantlon, Kathy Delaney, Barbara Fife, Betty McNeill, Jeanne Poore, Donna Lynn Thomas, and Susan Thorup all pitched in to turn my virtual quilts into real quilt tops. Jeanne Zyck, Theresa Ward, and Freda Smith worked their machine-quilting magic. And last, but certainly not least, many bindings were stitched by Debi Schrader. To each of you: Your work is exceptional, your efforts are appreciated, and your friendship is treasured. Thank you!

Lamar Sims, my vocal coach and friend, who is one of the most creative, musically talented, intellectually brilliant, and "real" people I know. I appreciate your wisdom and your insightfulness. Reminiscent of a song, I can say with both intellectual honesty and from the depths of my being that, because I know you, I have truly been changed "for good" (and for the better).

My sons, Michael Ashton Bentley and Steven Richard Seib: Thanks for all the joy, laughter, and creative parenting opportunities you have brought—and continue to bring—to my life. I adore you both, and I love being your mom! My daughter-in-law, Amanda: It is wonderful having you in our family. My grandkids: Connor, Sara, and Vayda, you add such sparkle to my life. I love you *all* so very much!

Jeff Seib, my husband of nearly a quarter-century: Thank you for the way you love, support, and encourage me through every adventure. You never complain about all the fabric I bring home or the threads that are strewn about the house. You cheerfully make meals and do laundry when I'm up to my eyeballs in a project that must be completed. You ooooh and ahhhh over every quilt *and* offer valuable feedback. You are a fabulous quilt schlepper and car organizer. Your patience and kindness know no bounds. I love you. Longer!

About the Author

Photo by Norma Elgan

Kelly's romance with quiltmaking began in the mid-1980s, though it didn't fully blossom until a decade later when both her sons were in school. Then, in addition to "quiltmaker," she soon added "quilting instructor" and "long-arm quilter" to her list of preferred activities. As a self-described "pragmatic quiltmaker," Kelly approaches quilt design and construction with a knowledge of and appreciation for the theoretical and a penchant for the practical. She continually seeks and implements efficient shortcuts that do not compromise the quality of the finished product. Her midlife realization that she truly may not live long enough to use all of her fabric stash has propelled her into turbo quiltmaking mode, though it hasn't stopped her from adding to her stash. After all, the one who dies with the most fabric wins, right?

Kelly resides in Overland Park, Kansas, with her husband, Jeff Seib, and their miniature schnauzer, Shyma. She is mother to Michael and Steven, and Nana to Connor, Sara, and Vayda. In addition to her quiltmaking passion, Kelly enjoys singing with the Kansas City Women's Chorus, traveling, being mesmerized by the ocean, cooking, playing pinochle, and spending time with family and friends.